MW01194888

Mentally STRONG™:
Against All Odds, We Choose

By Drs. Francis and Cristi Bundukamara

`

Authors: Francis and Cristi Bundukamara
Project: Mentally STRONG™: Against All Odds, We Choose

Copyright © 2018 Francis and Cristi Bundukamara
NOTICE: IF THIS MATERIAL IS INTERCEPTED, IT IS PROTECTED BY COPYRIGHT AND ANY BREACH OF INTELLECTUAL PROPERTY OR CONFIDENTIALITY WILL BE PROSECUTED TO THE FULL EXTENT OF THE LAW. DESTROY THIS COPY WITHOUT READING FURTHER.

Permission to Quote Copyright and Trademark Information

All Scripture quotations, unless otherwise indicated, are taken from the Holy Bible, New International Version®, NIV®. Copyright ©1973, 1978, 1984, 2011 by Biblica, Inc.™ used by permission of Zondervan. All rights reserved worldwide. www.zondervan.com The "NIV" and "New International Version" are trademarks registered in the United States Patent and Trademark Office by Biblica, Inc.™

Table of Contents

Prologue

We believe you too can be Mentally STRONG™, and pray you are encouraged and inspired by our story. During the midst of our hardship, God taught us ways to continue to develop our mental strength, through processing, organizing and making positive decisions to never give up. Our reason for writing the details of our personal story, is the earnest hope that processing our story together will help to heal some of the emotional pain, dissolve our initial anger at God, heal our broken hearts, strengthen our marriage and allow us to say with confidence I am Mentally STRONG™.

When we were married we faced the usual struggles most young couples encounter, and we were ready for the challenge. Our diverse family includes two biological mixed-race children, five adopted children, and the lovable, determined, but stubborn African-born grandfather. A devastating, rare, and difficult to diagnose genetic disorder struck us unexpectedly, challenging our view of life, our mental strength, and our faith in God. Life is filled with joy and pain, in varying degrees for different people.

We have had our share of both and we recognize that people are immensely resilient, and we all have the choice to find mental strength, to love, to hope, to persevere, and to never give up. We also appreciate that while we have experienced heart-wrenching setbacks through the years, our family has relied on each other for comfort and support, and we are all mentally stronger.

We are devoted followers of Christ, and while the important foundation our faith has given us will be reflected in our story, this book is not an explicitly Christian work by any means. Our story is not an attempt to proselytize for converts, but is a human story, easily embraced by all people alike. While our story clearly portrays our relationship with God through Jesus Christ, it is *our* story, and you are simply invited to share in our triumphs and struggles.

The title, *Mentally STRONG™ Against all Odds: We Choose*, reflects two major themes: choosing to stay mentally strong in the face of adversity; and overcoming against all odds. Our family lives by these two maxims. The first has given us and our children the assurance that we truly *can* choose our state of mind, and govern our emotions. Choosing this mindset has also enabled us to face each day with the peace needed to make painfully difficult emotional decisions. The second has given us the strength to persevere when we seem to be facing impossible odds. Our determined refusal to never give up in times of great stress and adversity has been a key factor in keeping our family focused on what must be accomplished, rather than being paralyzed by fear.

Cristi developed a self-help technique called Choice Mapping™. Choice Mapping™ is a simple and practical technique for developing mental strength. Empowering individuals to organize thought processes and develop a personal algorithm for perseverance. If you are interested in learning about Choice Mapping™: a formula to say "I am Mentally STRONG™" visit www.mentally-strong.com

We are the Bundukamara's, and this is our story...

Chapter One: Reggie

Reggie was having a bad day. I was concerned but not worried, because he'd had days like this before. I watched his chest rise and fall, trying to decide whether to attach the oxygen supply. He seemed okay now. A slight smile replaced my frown as I remembered he had people coming over today for his favorite therapy, which we began calling Reggie Therapy years prior. Reggie Therapy helped the participants as much as it soothed Reggie. He always felt better after the hands-on activity. He also enjoyed seeing the friends and family who came to our home to lay hands on his organs and muscles to promote improved function. Noticing his breathing had become labored again I slipped the oxygen mask over his mouth and nose and slowly turned the valve. I knelt next to him and held his hand. My seventeen-year-old boy. My baby, who I loved so much, it was often painful to watch him look so uncomfortable. I contemplated whether I should take him to the hospital, but decided to wait and see how he felt after the Reggie Therapy.

My mind drifted back to the day my husband, Bundy, and I decided to become parents. I smiled, as I always do when I recall seeing Reggie for the first time. I remembered the love I felt for him when we later dedicated him to God in covenant baptism. I thought of his first words, then his first tentative steps, followed by boundless energy as he raced around our home climbing onto and over everything. I could see again the precocious, active little big brother, pushing his sister around the yard on their bicycle. I snapped back to the present as the nurse approached us. I focused on Reggie in alarm, but he was fine. I considered again taking him to the emergency room, just in case, but I couldn't tell what the cause of the problem was—he didn't even have a fever.

The frustration with deciding whether to take him to the hospital was that the staff there often didn't know what to do with very special needs kids. They always automatically placed Reggie in ICU, but he very often bounced back quickly and we were stuck there for up to three days. Afraid of liability, doctors are reluctant to discharge too quickly in case his condition deteriorates after we leave. The volunteers who perform Reggie Therapy gave him the nickname, "The Rubberband Man" because of his ability to bounce back from some critical situations. I considered all the medical equipment in our home to treat Reggie, the full-time nursing staff to attend to him, as well as the fact I'm a nurse, and felt maybe I was over-reacting to the situation.

This reminded me of the bad day Reggie had a few years ago, when we were being interviewed for an article in the March 2014 edition of *People Magazine*. There I was, holding Reggie after multiple exhausting seizures, trying to look good for the photographer and give the writer the attention he required. Pose, click click, re-position, click click… while I tried to answer questions about seizures and cannabis professionally. The article was titled "Medical Marijuana: Kids Fight Seizures—With Pot." Reggie was fourteen at the time and it was exciting to be in a magazine article, though it wasn't really about us. The article detailed how some families face the current reality of having to leave their homes and move across the country so they can legally gain access to cannabis treatment. It didn't help that Reggie was having a bad day, and his condition didn't improve during the three-to-four-hour interview and photo shoot. I silently prayed cannabis would be the miracle we needed for Reggie. The article called Reggie's illness a "rare genetic disorder," and when Reggie's dad and I first read those words, it seemed to be an extremely simplified term for the disorder that has turned our lives upside down. This illness is what drives us to fight, and cannabis is what brought us to Colorado.

I observed Reggie for a while and felt relieved that he appeared much better now. He was breathing more easily and his vital signs were good. It seemed I was being overly anxious. I continued with my day but kept Reggie near me, alert for any signs of change in his state. As a nurse, I am trained to recognize an emergency. The month after Reggie was featured in the magazine article, he spent some time in the ICU for pneumonia. I had recognized the symptoms and took him to the emergency room. The month after Reggie's bout of pneumonia I could see he was in severe pain, and though I couldn't tell what the cause was, I drove him to the hospital. Even though the staff told me they couldn't find any reason for pain on the CT scan, I didn't regret taking him in, because if I feel I should take him to the hospital I do. Reggie's condition today didn't appear to be an emergency, but I couldn't shake my uncertainty regarding whether I should take him to the hospital or not.

I kept thinking about all the previous emergencies. Reggie was in moderate pain most of the time, so pain wasn't new to him. His pain tolerance levels were high, but the week following the CT scan we could see he was really suffering. Unable to control his reaction to the severe pain, he would scream when it became too much. My anger rises when I remember returning to the hospital with Reggie the following week to be told the previous week's CT scan revealed a fractured femur head. When the second doctor viewed the original CT scan, the fracture in the femur was clearly evident but it had been missed by the previous doctor. What had been a fracture *then* was a complete break a week later. To say we were super pissed at the obvious negligence is an understatement... or was it *my* fault for not taking him back? Reggie is extremely sensitive to anaesthesia, so any surgery is hard for him. He experienced various complications during his rehabilitation after the hip surgery, and his muscles contracted, pulling his spine into a C form. We felt devastated by this turn of events because hip fractures can be extremely debilitating. Even though Reggie was just a young boy, his life changed after that operation.

I glanced over for the hundredth time that day to where he sat, hoping for one of his reassuring smiles, smiles which had become all too rare. Nothing warms our hearts like a smile from Reggie. We would sit at the edge of his bed after he had been for surgery, fervently praying, and waiting for him to wake up. When he opened his eyes and saw us sitting there, his cheerful, sunny smile always filled us with hope. His breathing was stable, so I removed the oxygen mask and kissed his forehead. He had been through so much over the past few years. I thought back to the PICC line that was inserted so we could intravenously administer his antibiotics at home. I also recalled the bi-monthly drive to Denver for a whole year so Reggie could receive his IVIG treatment (type of immune therapy)—which, fortunately, we were

`

later able to change to subcutaneous IG (SCIG) treatment at home. Then the Deep Brain Stimulation (DBS) surgery which had to be performed at Cook's Children's Hospital in Dallas, because Denver Children's Hospital told us Reggie's illness was too complex to perform the surgery there.

Each new therapy or course of medicine instilled renewed optimism in us, raising our hope that this would be the one to transform Reggie's life, and if not to heal him completely, to at least improve the quality of his life. We clung desperately to our hope that the DBS treatment would reduce the dystonia Reggie was experiencing, which caused involuntary and repetitive painful muscle contractions. Our hope was destroyed yet again when we realized there was absolutely no improvement in Reggie's dystonia attacks. We began to feel overwhelmed. It seemed as if there was nothing we could do to change things. We were grasping for hope at every turn, frantically wanting to believe in a miracle. I felt like I was holding my breath while fighting off negative thoughts... *He can't come back from this, you're losing your son.* Bundy didn't understand the procedures or how they would help Reggie, so he was scared all the time. All we could do was rely on medical advancements to make Reggie better. We chose to believe this was in God's plan and to never give up. We decided that in the worst case scenario, if nothing helped, the accumulated information could at least be used to help research this disorder. This thought caused me to reflect on an emotionally charged (now slightly edited) Facebook™ statement I posted, after a non-believing friend suggested we were wasting our time and energy:

> "It has been brought to my attention that some people think my fight against this disorder is futile; that I'm prolonging the inevitable and causing suffering. I can assure you, I'm not in denial, and I understand limitations. I can also assure you that quality of life is my goal, and that we are not afraid of death. We know without a shadow of a doubt that our relationship is eternal in Heaven. I also know that God could provide a miracle, and I will continue to pray that way. I refuse to let a negative, hopeless, dependent culture dictate my fight."

We intentionally chose to think positively. Some days it was a battle of the mind. On those days we willfully chose to go through life's motions. Our hearts hurt and we were scared, but we chose not to let our hearts affect our actions. Just when we were tired and wanted to give up, Reggie would have a good day and smile at us. On those days my heart soared, and the determination to fight was strengthened. We had pinned our hope on the DBS treatment succeeding, and our hope was dashed once again. The bitterness of the result was alleviated to some degree when we discovered the DBS treatment had at least reduced the frequency of Reggie's seizures. Before the DBS, Reggie experienced three to six seizures every third day, like clock-work. The DBS stopped the cycle, and he would only have seizures a couple of times a month. There is no medical explanation though, for why the placement of the DBS should improve his seizures. Noting it was almost three p.m., I moved Reggie to his room and prepared him for his therapy session.

The sound of laughter and youthful chatter approaching made me turn my head towards the front door. The Reggie addicts, as we affectionately call them, had arrived to give Reggie his therapy. They trooped into Reggie's room after we shared warm greetings and hugs. The delight on Reggie's face at seeing his friends and family who had come out to make him feel better was the highlight of my day. I saw the same pleasure when we used to take him horseback riding, and I recalled how his face had been alive with joy when we were on the Disney Cruise he was granted from the Make-A-Wish Foundation™. Water slides, roller coasters, and bike races also light up Reggie's face so vibrantly that you can't help feeling his excitement. I could see today's therapy made Reggie feel better, and after everyone had left I tested his vital signs, and they were perfect. His breathing was even, and he was relaxed. I was also feeling less anxious, and better about my decision not to take him to the hospital.

After saying goodbye to the day nurse at six p.m., I returned to where Reggie lay and saw he had begun struggling with his breathing again. I fitted the oxygen mask to his face and watched him closely. I wrestled again with the decision to take him to the hospital, only now things had changed. Oxygen can't be administered in my car, so we would have to call 911 to take Reggie to the emergency room. I watched his breathing, deciding if this was an emergency. He seemed fine, and I knew if I called 911, I would have to exaggerate the description of Reggie's condition for them to come out here. I needed someone to help me with the decision, so I called for Bundy, who was playing games on the PlayStation™. Bundy came through and I asked him what we should do. Bundy felt I was best equipped to make the decision, so it was up to me. The stress of the day's anxiety hit me at once, and I screamed at Bundy that he was no help at all. It may have been an irrational response, but I just needed someone to help me make the decision, one way or the other.

I paced up and down next to Reggie's bed, my mind in turmoil over what to do. I didn't feel this was an emergency, but Reggie was still having difficulty breathing. I finally made the decision to call 911. Just then I heard my phone signal a message received. I picked it up and was surprised to see the message was from Heather, a close friend of mine who also has a special needs child. The message informed me Heather was coming over to see me. I checked the time and saw it was almost ten p.m. Heather runs the Realm of Caring Foundation™, as well as taking care of her own special needs child. We're both super busy, and so even though we are close friends we rarely have the time to drive across town to visit, especially not at ten in the evening. I explained the situation and told her I was going to call 911. She said I should call, but insisted she was coming over anyway. Heather told me she was at home, getting ready for bed when God told her to come to our home.

I called 911 and Bundy went outside to make sure the rescue workers knew which house was ours. While we waited Reggie began to hyperventilate, so I decided to test the level of oxygen in his blood. Trembling, I fitted a pulse oximeter to Reggie's finger but couldn't get it to work properly. The rescue workers arrived and Bundy showed them in. I was still having difficulty getting the pulse ox to work properly and was becoming increasingly anxious. Heather arrived as the rescue workers attached their machine to Reggie, and I realized at that moment just how serious his condition was. Knowing the rescue workers were in a better frame of mind than me to save my son, I left the room, and I started praying. When I pray in those situations I don't think about God's answer. It's almost like an unconscious prayer because I'm in a state of shock. My shock prayers are just… oh God, please… and I hold my breath...

Source: © 2018 Francis and Cristi Bundukamara
Cristi and Reggie

Chapter Two: Honeymoon Years

We love to tell the story of how we met. You see, Cristi and I met in jail. We then pause and let their minds wonder about which one of us was in jail. The truth is, Cristi was a nurse at a juvenile detention facility called, *Everglades Academy*. I began teaching at the facility after I had moved to Florida. I was drawn to Cristi by her friendly, energetic personality, and I won't deny being physically attracted to her. We got along well, so we soon became good friends, but Cristi was a Christian and I was not. Besides, I had a fiancé back in Maryland.

One day Cristi invited me to a Christian music concert and I was hesitant, but figured, *Yeah, okay.* I loved being with her so it was a no-brainer but I had no idea my life would completely change that night. The irony is, as much as that night is engraved into my memory, if anyone asked me about the show, I couldn't tell them a thing. All I heard was the message of God's love and redeeming grace booming through the song lyrics. In that moment I instantly realized I was alive for a purpose. Right there, my life was changed, and I made the decision at that concert to follow

Jesus and fulfill the purpose He had created me for.

Cristi and I loved spending time together but we did so discreetly to prevent others from forming the wrong impression. We truly were being faithful to God and our principles, but people may not have understood our close friendship. I was never forward with Cristi, but one night, I tried to kiss her. She surprised me by saying "no". I was a popular guy—a football player—and wasn't used to being refused but instead of turning me away from Cristi, her commitment drew me closer. Cristi wasn't some ordinary church girl, and her testimony of knowing God through Christ had a powerful effect on me.

You see, Cristi was previously known as a "fun bad girl." A strong-willed child, and a rebellious teen, who moved out at sixteen, got pregnant, had an abortion, experimented with drugs, joined the army, and drank a lot. She even claims to have driven her parents to the Lord. A few days after the devastating Category 5 Hurricane Andrew hit their home in South Florida, Cristi heard an unconventional gospel presentation: "Here is a revolver.

Would you put a bullet in here and play Russian roulette? That's what you are doing with your eternal life when you play with God's word!" Apparently that's the day it all changed, and by the time we met she was abstinent of drugs, excessive alcohol, and sex for four years. Her strong-willed, fun, outgoing personality never changed, and I was drawn to that.

Over the next few weeks I read the Bible, eager to understand Cristi's motivations. I began to realize how God wanted me to live, and I discovered some passages where God calls a husband and wife "one flesh."[1] In that moment I suddenly knew my fiancé was not the woman God had planned for me to spend my life with. It was a revelation! The more I considered it, the stronger the certainty I felt in my heart. One night I was reading the Bible alone and came across 1 Corinthians 13. I realized at that moment, I did not love my fiancé.

Without hesitation I made the decision to end the relationship with my fiancé. Right away I scheduled a trip to

---

1   Genesis 2:24; Mark 10:8

Maryland, and braced myself for the difficult task of telling her. When I examined my motives, of course I had strong feelings for Cristi... but this was not why I ended my relationship with my fiancé. I simply knew she was not the right woman for me.

She was terribly upset when I told her, and understandably so. We had been together for ten years. Her reaction made it especially hard on me, and while I really felt for her, I just knew it wasn't the lifetime, covenant relationship God wanted me to join myself to. I struggled a little at first, but my sister helped me through that period. And, of course, there was no guarantee Cristi and I would end up together. But I was determined to do the right thing in God's view.

As I got off the plane on my return from Maryland, I saw Cristi waiting for me. By the joy and excitement I felt at seeing her again, I knew Cristi was the one woman I could love forever. Incredibly, Cristi said she felt the same way about me and soon after we began to date, we knew we would be married. It was like a fairy-tale. We often say, we felt God's love through each other.

I had been raised to ask a girl's father for her hand in marriage, but I had, up to that point, had very little interaction with Cristi's father. So, when he asked me to join him and his sons at a *Promise Keepers* convention in the Redlands area I was surprised but pleased. I grinned to myself as I decided that attending a convention of believing men committed to keeping their promise to God and their wives was the perfect time to ask Cristi's father for her hand in marriage.

My heart leapt at his response. I knew God had orchestrated my marriage when Cristi's father, who had known me only a short time, agreed to my request without hesitation. Bear in mind, a marriage between a black man from Africa and a local blonde girl who had only known each other for a short time would be a surprise to any family, but there were fewer issues surrounding our color difference than you would think. Fewer issues, but not absent entirely.

Being African, and especially from Sierra Leone, my cultural upbringing made me different. It was instilled in us to do things the right way once we moved to America. For example, we were always reminded to be aware of the time of day, so we could answer the phone correctly. "Good evening, who is calling?" If we just said a casual "Hi," in person or over the phone, we were beaten. Respect was ingrained in us, and this impressed others as very mannerly. In addition, I was the golden child growing up, since I was the youngest. I was going to pass on the African name, so it was important that I was doing things right.

Being half royalty, it was understandable my parents wanted me to marry an African woman. Well, not just a black woman, nor just an African woman. They wanted me to marry a woman from Sierra Leone. There's a significant difference. I have come to realize that people from Sierra Leone are sometimes arrogant. It seems as if they don't like anybody else, especially other Africans. They give them that smile—you know that smile, "Oh, how you doing?"—but that's all. Then they talk disdainfully about the person. My mother must have known I would look like a mean individual, so she made extra effort to teach me to share, and to "kill people with kindness." I believe that is what has kept

20

me going through the years; it even allowed me to share Christ more easily. Cristi's family believed they had no issues with people of other races, but I felt there was some difficulty truly wanting an inter-racial marriage for their daughter... I couldn't blame them, my dad felt the same way. In addition to the few race challenges, we faced a few others. We hadn't known each other very long and there were even concerns that we had not had sex. One of Cristi's aunts went out of her way to counsel us, hoping to dissuade us from marrying so quickly by asking, "Would you buy a pair of shoes you haven't tried on?" We found this very funny and still laugh about it till this day. We remained abstinent till marriage, trusting God's blessing.

Maybe I made it sound easier than it was, but I can understand how a family doesn't simply give their daughter to a man they have known less than six months. It took a while. Trust me, it took a while... Cristi believes it wasn't as bad as I remember, but there were some moments. I don't know what the breakthrough was, maybe powerful prayer, or possibly just because I'm a lovable guy. But one day, it all just came together and I became family.

Cristi's dad agreed to our marriage in June and we planned to be married in December that year. It was quick, but we wanted to do things right, and we felt December, being a month with greater spiritual relevance because of Christmas, was a good month to be married. But December was not to be!

You see, we found a townhouse that we wanted to purchase together, but didn't want to live together before we were married. Even though Cristi's mom was concerned about the speed with which the relationship was progressing, she asked us a simple question followed by wise advice: "Do you love each other?" When we replied that we certainly did love one another, she asked, "Then why wait?" We realized Cristi's mom was right, and on July 25th, the following month, we were married at Redlands Community Church, our local fellowship!

During those honeymoon years we thrived, with everything seeming to fall into place. Cristi and I knew we were soul mates, mostly because we could feel God's love shining through each other. We knew that if we continued doing good and obeying God, He would continue to bless us in every area—spiritually, physically, and emotionally. It was blissful and life was great, although not necessarily easy. Even though we were both professionals, we didn't have much money. I also came from an affluent family and had no idea how to be frugal, so Cristi had the fun task of teaching me how to make our money go further. Poor Cristi even paid for her own wedding ring, and we had to delay going on our honeymoon until the following year. We thought those years were tough because we were living hand to mouth, paycheck to paycheck, but we were praying a lot, as people do when they are struggling. And we continually saw evidence of God looking after us, even to cover urgent expenses. I remember one time we needed exactly $181.25 for something, and were extremely anxious and didn't know where we were going to get the money. Then I went to the mailbox and found an unexpected insurance check for precisely $181.25! Who else but God could orchestrate such precise relief? So those were good years. In many ways, those were the easiest years.

Then our financial situation improved when my application was accepted as a full time teacher and football coach at the local high school. It was my dream job! My build allowed me to play offense and defense in my football-playing years, so I knew how to train the kids for both types of play. I excelled at the job, and our team went on to go nine years undefeated. This, and my ability to have mentoring relationships with teens naturally made me a firm favorite in the community.

For quite some time at that point, Cristi had been feeling God was calling us to become parents. While in church on Mother's Day, a message on the value of a mother's contribution to our lives really touched our hearts. We decided that very day to stop taking birth control, and to embark on the joyful but daunting experience of becoming parents.

Within months we were elated to discover Cristi was pregnant. Pregnancy is a wonderful, challenging, and stressful time for any soon-to-be-parent, and it was the same for us. We did everything new parents usually do—watching what Cristi ate, making sure we carefully heeded the doctor's advice, never missing a checkup... our little baby boy was going to a perfect addition to our lives! After the exciting time preparing for his birth, our son, Reggie, was born on May 5th, 1999.

Only parents can know the delight of holding in your arms a perfect little person, who reflects both of you, and yet is his own little individual self. Just as during the pregnancy, we wanted to do everything right, so Cristi stayed home to nurse Reggie and provide everything he needed. Boy, did we feel so blessed! Reggie was a healthy, active child who brought endless joy to our hearts and developed normally according to all the milestones for his age. Cristi was the perfect Christian wife and mother, and we were so confident and assured of God's leading and protection in our lives. In September that year, we dedicated our firstborn son to God in covenant baptism. I was awed by the depth and power of that moment of complete spiritual submission to God. We fully believed in His protection and blessing over our precious son.

We wasted no time in building our family, and Reggie was

a year old when our beautiful daughter, Miah, was born. We couldn't have felt more blessed with such a perfect new addition to our family. My little Irish twins—that's a term for children born exactly one year apart. We couldn't wait to take our new baby home, and when Cristi and Miah were discharged we packed up and headed home. Life was going so well!

When we got home, as I opened the front door of our home, the lower level was completely flooded! A pipe had burst while we were at the hospital, gushing water likely for days, leaving the entire bottom floor of our home unusable and dangerous. We knew we had no choice but to adapt. We went to Cristi's mother's house and stayed in a travel trailer in the back yard. Needless to say, caring for an infant and a toddler in a trailer was a challenge, but we chose not to be overwhelmed. Instead we used the insurance money we received for the water damage to pay for the repairs and renovation of the townhouse, and we sold it. The profit we made allowed us to start building our dream home on a piece of family land next to Cristi's mom in Redland. This is a tranquil agricultural zone on the outskirts of Miami and we rejoiced at how even our difficulties were being turned into blessings!

Our blessings still came at some price though. While our dream home was being built, we continued to live in a trailer parked outside Cristi's mom's house. Actually, we slept in the trailer and spent most of our time in the house with Cristi's mom. It was rough living out of a trailer for the two years it took to complete our home, but the upside was that grandma was able to spend a lot of time with her grandchildren, which suited her perfectly.

We managed the building contracting ourselves, meaning, as owners, we hired contractors to complete the different stages of building. Doing it this way allowed us to build according to the budget we could afford at the time. The overall project cost a lot less too. In May, 2002, our perfect home was completed, and we moved into our brand new home with our delightful two children. We couldn't have been happier but didn't know life was about to get even more exciting!

Cristi is a really resourceful woman, and sometimes I can't figure out why she loves me so much. Then I look at how Christ loves us, all of us, no matter what; and it's easier to understand how she loves me... no matter what. Cristi is also a very driven woman, and is always open to new opportunities to help other people. Not too long after we moved into our new home, a conference was held at our church for the *Mission to the World* organization. During this conference, Cristi and I both felt a powerful calling from God to enter the mission field. We immediately approached the elders of our church to let them know of our willingness to obey this calling we felt to missions. The elders granted their support and we contacted *Mission to the World* to apply. Having the willingness to do missions isn't enough though. Mission work isn't easy, and people doing mission work represent God and the organization sending them. So understandably, a careful check for suitability is required, as well as a clear understanding of what to expect and what will be expected from you when going on missions. We were interviewed extensively, and went through comprehensive psychological testing. As confident of the outcome as we were, we were still thrilled when we were accepted.

Enthusiastic to start doing the work we felt called to as soon as possible, we excitedly notified our church of the outcome. Imagine the shock we felt when they withdrew their approval of our application to *Mission to the World*. We were stunned and bewildered by their reaction, feeling puzzled and bitterly disappointed. Had we misunderstood God, whom we felt sure was calling us to missions? If so, why had we been approved by the mission organization? We discussed it and prayed about it, and came to the firm conclusion that God wanted us to be involved in missions. It's no easy thing to change churches; we were married in that church, and I taught Sunday school and worked with the youth. We had dedicated our eldest child in covenant baptism to the Lord in this church. We felt uncertain and confused, but if we were to move forward, we had no option but to find a church that would support our calling.

We found a new church within our denomination, and

made known to the leadership our intention to enter the mission field. We advised them of our application, and our acceptance by *Mission to the World*, and to our delight, they were supportive and agreed to send us. Finally, we could start the work God had called us to do! We got started right away, with most of the work involving planning and organizing trips locally, in the United States. We would then go on expeditions to train local people on a strategy for ministering to street children. As soon as we began, we knew we were in God's perfect will. Our hearts flooded with joy and spiritual rewards as we made a difference in the lives of these tragically underprivileged kids.

The strategy was training locals to first find a house in the community where the street children lived. The house was then equipped like a family home, and opened up to the street kids every day for breakfast, showers, clean clothes, Bible study, and lunch. In the evenings it was closed. The kids could never sleep there, but they were provided with a place to hang out, receive meals, and make use of the facilities when needed. The ultimate goal was to teach them about Christ and His love for them, get them off the street, and usually, to get them off drugs in the process (it's horrific how most street children are being victimized with sex trafficking, and performing in porn films; and how many of them are addicted to drugs, just to cope with their situation).

What more could any young family ask for? Soul mates in a marriage. Perfect children in a perfect home, with the whole family part of a perfect calling to help street children. Cristi and I affectionately refer to this time in our lives as "the honeymoon years."

Source: © 2018 Francis and Cristi Bundukamara
Bundy, Reggie, and Miah

Chapter Three: African Son

"So, shoot me!" I challenged the man pointing a handgun at my chest. My pulse was racing but in the back of my mind I knew that if he did pull the trigger, he would probably only aim for my shoulder. I was ready for a bullet, knowing how crazy this guy could be... after all, he *was* my father, so maybe some of his craziness had rubbed off on me, because I had actually just dared him to shoot me.

"You think I won't do it, boy?" he asked me, looking into my eyes, speaking in a measured voice, as if I were daring him to shoot a raccoon.

"I know you won't do it!" I gambled hopefully. "I know you won't do it because you're African and I'm your son—I'm the one who's going to pass on your family name... and you're going to shoot me?" We stared at one another like they do in those old Western movies. Then I asked him again, "So, are you gonna shoot?" He stared at me for a few more intense seconds, and then he just put the gun down. Now, that's the kind of man I was dealing with.

My father was a fiercely independent and constantly displaying his characteristic vigor, Moses Abram Bundukamara lived life on his own terms, we later lovingly called him Pop Pops.

I was eighteen years old when this gun incident took place. We were living in Maryland, and if truth be told, I don't even know what argument caused him to pull out his gun. I don't recall this particular disagreement but what I do remember is how volatile his personality was—with my father, everything escalated quickly. And all I ever wanted was to be a part of him, so I would match emotion with emotion; if he showed anger, I would be angry. When he acted crazy, I would do the same. I wanted to be like him when I was growing up, and he was angry a lot of the time, so I ended up acting angry too, and we fought a lot.

When I was born, my parents lived in Washington, D.C. We moved to the suburbs when I was about three, to Silver Spring, Maryland, in Montgomery County... where the rich people lived. Pop Pops tried to raise us as Muslims, but my mother was Episcopalian, and she won over, so we identified as Episcopalian or Methodist. When I would cry, my father would say my tears took me farther away from God. Our parents worked different shifts, and so us children had a lot of responsibilities placed on us at an early age.

Pop Pops was a lively character, who would throw out classic African anecdotes, which he used as an antidote for our misbehavior. When I did something wrong he would often correct me with an African saying. When I occasionally stayed out late at night, he would reference an old story concerning one of his cousins, who had been murdered after staying out all night, saying "Busybody die on street! Not in the house." When I acted grown up he would tell me, "You think you're a man? Me and your mother were doing things well before you were born, so don't think you're a man." When one of us asked for a cold drink he would often reply, "Thirsty? Swallow your spit!" What made these quirks of his so funny was that he said them in his distinctly African accent. Pop Pops was very proud of his African roots.

I was raised by a Sierra-Leonean man who believed he was of royal descent. My family is originally from Kono District, which is divided into fourteen chiefdoms, and my grandfather was one of these district chiefs, so maybe he was of royal linage. They killed royalty there during the civil war, and I would have been a part of that, so it's a good thing I was born an American.

Pop Pops was a loving man, but he only told me three times he loved me and that he was proud of me. Each time was after a significant accomplishment of mine. During his later years, he lost his home and became poorer. My mom was diagnosed with kidney disease in 1980, and she battled against it for ten years before passing. Pop Pops had to retire early to take care of my mom when she became too sick to look after herself. My mom died in 1991, the year I completed my undergraduate degree. My parents had been married for thirty years, so her death sent my dad over the edge. Pop Pops really struggled without her. He was no longer financially stable, and when my mother died, everything started falling apart.

From 1986 to 1991 I was an undergrad at Salisbury State University. That's where I got my nickname: Bundy. That's where I played football. That's where I became a man! I got my undergraduate degree in Liberal Studies. My minor subjects were sociology, psychology, and Spanish. I studied Spanish in high school too. I married Cristi in 1997, and we bought a townhouse to live in. I completed my Masters in 1998. It was during that year we went back to my home town in Maryland to visit Pop Pops. The bank had repossessed our childhood home and Pop Pops was in a nursing home. Mom had been gone for seven years, and even though I wasn't close to him, I could tell he wasn't doing well.

Pop Pops had a narcissistic personality. He bragged about being a retired research pharmacist who held a number of Ph.D.'s, and who was a royal personage back in Sierra Leone. Seeing him didn't bring to mind many fond memories, and I realized I still harbored a lot of anger against him. Cristi was confused by my attitude because she came from a family where the elders always helped to take care of their grandchildren.

In the end, Cristi convinced me; you don't just leave one of your parents in a nursing home—you care for them. I would have to give up my childhood anger and accept my responsibility to take care of Pop Pops. So we moved him into our home. We were living in Florida at the time, in the townhouse we had bought. Pop Pops was seventy-eight years old, and he had been diagnosed with chronic obstructive pulmonary disease (COPD.) We were told it was progressive, and we assumed, due to his apparent frailty, that he only had a few years left to live.

Even though he seemed frail when we took him in, he immediately found the strength to start arguing with me. He refused to contribute to the household and spent his money on unknown things. Cristi and I agreed not to let this affect our relationship with him, but one day in 1999 things took a bad turn.

Pop Pops became so angry with me that his rage seemed almost psychotic. He attacked me with a knife. Again, I don't even recall our disagreement—Pop Pops' temper would just flare suddenly. Cristi was so scared she called the police. They took

38

`

Pop Pops to a psychiatric hospital for a couple of days, and when he was discharged he disappeared to Africa, to the Sierra Leone civil war.

Pop Pops later described the war, saying, "They were like crabs in a crab pot, all trying to pull the other crabs back into the pot to get on top—to save themselves." Later we received a message from the American Embassy in Nigeria, advising us to wire money for Pop Pops so he could come back home. Pop Pops had apparently gotten into a civil war altercation, and had been forced to flee to Nigeria. Having confirmed the authenticity of the request, we wired the money. Pop Pops was back living with us, and we were grateful to have him back home. By this time, Reggie and Miah were born, we were living in our new home, and I had my dream job teaching and coaching football, and I was working on furthering my education.

Source: © 2018 Francis and Cristi Bundukamara
Pop Pops and Reggie

Chapter Four: Adoption

Our long-awaited dream home was finally complete, and we were excited and eager to move in. The *new-homee* smell of fresh paint and everything new made the stress of living in what felt like a mobile box for two years all worthwhile. Bundy had his dream job at South Dade School, and was a valued and respected teacher there, well-known for caring about the students and taking an interest in their lives. He could often be found counseling students on campus, sometimes for hours.

Having noticed a female student, Nidra, appeared anxious and emotional at school one day, Bundy ambled over and sat down next to her. When she looked up, he offered to listen if she wanted to talk. With tears streaming down her cheeks, the story of how a disagreement with her alcoholic mother had resulted in her being kicked out of the house poured out of her. She confided between sobs that she had nowhere to live, and was likely to end up in a shelter.

Bundy usually displays his emotion on each end of the

spectrum; usually he is a happy, lovable guy but he can also get really angry. Fortunately he is a lot more happy than angry, but there is a sensitive side to him that couldn't bear to see the girl in this predicament. Sensing I would agree, he offered her a room in our home until she graduated. Our large new home had enough living space for an extra person, and I readily agreed to her staying with us. When Bundy told Nidra, her expression was a mixture of stunned surprise and relieved gratitude at his offer for us to take her in. Packing the few items she owned into our car, we moved Nidra into her room that afternoon, then gave her the chance to settle in. We saw our home as a gift from God, and we were determined to share it as such. It felt wonderful to be able to help a vulnerable young person in such need.

Taking Nidra into our family was an opportunity to show God's love to someone who desperately needed to be loved and supported, so our intention was to care for, and guide, this young girl who needed a chance in life. She was almost eighteen, and we wanted to help her get on her feet, to support her until she was able to go out and face life on her own. God had blessed us, and we chose to pass that blessing on to someone else. As we soon discovered, this sweet, introverted girl with a sarcastic sense of humor was also an organized and independent young woman who didn't hesitate to take charge of a situation. Avoiding work is not a part of Nidra's character, and we noted that giving up on something she has set her heart on achieving never enters her mind. An underlying anxiety, concealed by Nidra's strong personality and calm exterior, was acknowledged only to herself in private tears. Pop Pops also really liked Nidra. She was accommodating, helpful, and very easy to love, and she quickly became part of the family. When we chose to help Nidra finish high school and make the transition into adulthood, we had no idea we would grow to love her so wholeheartedly.

A few months later, in that same year, we received an unexpected visit from the pastor of our church. As we sat around the kitchen table drinking coffee, he tentatively inquired of us if we would be open to adopting a boy from the church, a boy we had known for many years. Cory and his brother grew up in their birthplace, Miami, and attended church with their aunt whenever

Child Protective Services would temporarily move them from their parents' house to their aunt's home. Eventually, their parents lost their parental rights due to substance abuse, and the children were formally placed in the care of their aunt. The pastor told us that Cory and his aunt had recently run into difficulties, and Cory had been put into a shelter. Cory had grown up alongside us in the church, and we knew him personally. Knowing Cory well, we chose to believe in him and in the potential we saw in him.

Cory's mom was an alcoholic and she just couldn't stay sober, so essentially Cory was left alone to care for himself and his younger brother. This tall, clean-cut boy had been coming to our church on and off with his aunt since he was a little kid, so the decision was a no-brainer. "Of course we'll adopt Cory," was our reply to the pastor. While Cory's brother remained in their aunt's care, we immediately began the foster-to-adopt process with Cory. He wasn't in the foster care system yet, so his adoption was processed pretty quickly. Within a year of living with us he was adopted as our son. I felt proud of adopting Cory, as if I was rescuing a child, fighting for someone who couldn't fight for himself. For Bundy it was simple, he believed the words of Jesus: "Whoever welcomes one of these little children in my name welcomes me..."[2] This was still in the honeymoon phase of our life.

Many cases where children leave home or are removed and placed into the foster care system in America are directly related to substance abuse. As was the case with both Nidra and Cory. This doesn't necessarily develop into physical abuse, but substance abuse by parents often leads to the neglect of their children. Once a family is listed in the Child Protective Services system, it's extremely difficult to be delisted. The parents are often victims of broader societal problems, which often lead to substance abuse and addiction. I'm not attempting to justify the parents' behavior—substance abuse is a choice—but once you're in the system it's tough to get out. Child Protective Services give parents a chance to correct the situation, but they have to be a hundred percent sober for three years, and must submit to being

---

2   Partial rendition of Mark 9:37

tested every month. Child Protective Services will call at the house at any time, and the way I understand it, if everything isn't perfect during this three-year period, the parents will ultimately lose their children.

Cory was a cheerful and intelligent kid, and immediately took to Reggie, spending a lot of time playing and interacting with him. He loved playing sports, and he joined the football team Bundy coached. They developed a really good relationship, and Bundy made the decision to mentor Cory and mold him into the best man he could be. During this period we realized Nidra was a definite part of our family, and our love for her was like the love we felt for our own children. She was already an adult, but we felt that we would love to adopt her as one of our own. When we asked her if she would like to be adopted into our family her answer was yes, but legally it was a bit trickier than Cory's adoption because she was an adult. We weren't able to adopt her at the same time as Cory, but her adoption did take place later.

Pop Pops called Cory "White Boy," and we have a

favorite story regarding our family's diversity and the impression we give in public. This incident occurred at the customs area of the Peruvian airport on a mission trip. Reggie and Miah were still toddlers, so I was carrying one and Nidra the other, with Bundy and Cory hauling all our luggage, including supplies for the ministry. I was holding everyone's passports, and Bundy and I were in front when we reached the bag-searching area. As is common practice with international customs at most airports, the bag search is determined randomly by pushing a button, which flashes a green light—pass through—or a red light—stop and have your bags searched. Pleased to see the green light flash when we pushed the button, we quickly hurried everyone through, except Cory, who had fallen behind with all the heavy luggage and supplies he was dragging. He tried to hurry through after us, but the customs official didn't associate this white boy with our mixed family and shouted, "Stop!"

Alarmed, Cory pointed to us and stated, "That's my family there! That's my family." Unfortunately, Cory was speaking English to a Spanish-speaking official.

The customs official shook his head and pointed to the button, "Push."

"No, but my family already went through," Cory pleaded with him.

Becoming annoyed, the official repeated his command more firmly, "Push the button!"

As we were already through and Cory was on his own, he had no choice but to push the button. The light flashed red.

"Passport!" the official demanded.

At this point we realized Cory had been separated from us, but the officials on our side adamantly insisted we were not allowed to go back once we had passed through customs. We tried to explain what had happened but couldn't make ourselves understood because of the language difference. Cory had way too many bags for one person, and no passport, so he was bundled off into a separate room for further investigation. He anxiously tried to explain that he was part of our family, but they didn't believe him because we looked like an African-American mixed family, and he was white. Eventually we found someone who could understand English and they clarified the situation for us, but it took over thirty minutes before we were reunited. For a fifteen-year-old boy in a foreign country it was a pretty scary episode, but we all joke about it today.

Reggie's personality was rapidly developing, he was hyper, and a really happy boy—a perpetual motion machine, with never a dull moment. Reggie's physical development was significantly above average, but we were noticing some deficiency in tasks that required him to sit still and pay attention. At the age of four Reggie was diagnosed with ADHD, which didn't really surprise us, but we were disappointed his IQ registered low on the scale, at eighty-two. This was the beginning of my endless research into both conventional and alternative treatments for whatever was going on with Reggie. After several years of diets and supplements, I finally consented to ADHD medication through first grade.

Cory was a cheerful teen who didn't blame his parents for the difficulties he had experienced in childhood. He would often help Reggie ride his bike, running alongside him in case he fell. Cory also taught Reggie to play golf, and one day on his backswing, Reggie accidentally hit Miah on the head, resulting in her needing seven stitches. This is still Miah's favorite story to this day.

Bundy and I never for a moment regretted adopting Nidra and Cory. They fit seamlessly into our family, and we felt encouraged to continue adopting kids who needed the care of a loving family. We registered with the foster-to-adopt program, and specified boys as the choice of children we wanted to adopt. I didn't mind adopting either girls or boys, but Bundy felt he would be better at nurturing and guiding boys through life. We envisioned filling our home with a little football team, but we soon found out that our plans are not always God's plans.

Source: © 2018 Francis and Cristi Bundukamara
Order From top left:
  Cory, Nidra, Miah, Bundy, Cristi, and Reggie

Chapter Five: The Siblings

I heard the phone vibrate before it rang. My heart beat a little faster when I saw the call was from Child Protective Services. *Is this it?*

I recognized the case worker's voice, "We have a twelve-year-old boy here. He has no problems, and in fact, he looks like he could be your biological child."

It was going so well with Nidra and Cory, Bundy and I felt called to continue adopting children who needed a loving home. We wanted a large family, but weren't certain of the exact number of children. Our plan was to adopt one child at a time over the course of a few years, and see where God led us. Bundy and I felt it ironic attending the required foster parenting course, as we had already adopted two children and had two of our own. We likewise completed the Post Traumatic Stress Disorder and Attachment Disorder classes, despite being trained in those fields as part of our work. It was only days after we were registered as eligible foster parents when the call arrived.

"Oh, and one other thing," the case worker added, "he has nowhere to sleep tonight." A requirement of potential foster parents is to have a room prepared for the child to sleep in. We had specified we would adopt only boys, as trauma generally has a greater effect on girls, and Bundy felt better equipped to raise boys. We took a little time to calm our nervous excitement, and to mentally and emotionally prepare ourselves, before leaving to bring our future son home. With bated breath we followed the case worker into a small room to meet him. Johnny was about five-foot-five, around a hundred pounds, and with his clear, light-brown complexion, he could have passed as Puerto Rican or biracial. He was sitting with two slightly younger girls, and his steady gaze seemed guarded and apprehensive as the case worker introduced us. I smiled warmly in an attempt to reassure him.

"Those are his sisters," the caseworker casually told us. "The three of them have never been separated, and they have nowhere to go either." I was flabbergasted to discover the children had been returned to foster care earlier that day without any warning by their previous adoptive mother, who simply stated she just couldn't do it anymore. It astounded me a person could tell children she loved them, let them call her mom for more than a year, then return them. We were prepared for one child, but how could we separate Johnny from his sisters and leave the girls there? Our imagined strategy was to adopt a string of boys; each one settling in before adopting the next. We envisioned a cheerful little football team running around our home, but we were to learn our plans are not always God's plans. Trusting in God, we decided to adopt Johnny and his two sisters. Almost immediately, we began the work of adding another two rooms to our home, during which time Johnny slept in Reggie's room and the girls shared with Miah.

Johnny and his sisters, Cristina, who was ten, and Kayla, who was a year younger, were three of nine children. Born to parents who were substance abusers, these siblings had lived in multiple foster homes, some worse than others, as we would later discover. They were born in Miami, and so went through the Miami foster care system. Johnny was a sweet boy with a distinctly male sense of humor who had a talent for drawing. Shy

55

and withdrawn, he was guarded with his emotions and kept a distance between himself and other people. He took to Reggie immediately though, and seemed content living with us, but it was more often than not difficult to read him. Cristina was more openly anxious, and worried about everything. Her clear, beautiful, cream-brown skin highlighted the mole above her left cheek bone. Kayla, in contrast, was animated, loud, and very happy. She was always ready to be a part, but was strong-willed, even as a child, and could be rebellious—just as I was at that age. Although both girls seemed sweet on the outside, Cristina was easier to reach, where Kayla was smart and manipulative.

I don't know if we would have agreed to accept all the children if we had been told there were three, but we may have, because I say yes way too often. The case worker manipulated us by failing to mention the girls when she called, then pulled on our heartstrings by showing us the three children together. Still, taking in all three kids made me feel powerful. Being a psychiatric nurse practitioner and Bundy a special needs teacher, I felt we were better prepared for this than most other people. God

56

had prepared and equipped us in advance for raising challenging and emotionally demanding children. I truly believed if we covered them in love and applied Godly discipline they would respond and grow into the adults they were meant to be. Boy, was I humbled. Bundy felt we were unstoppable; we would be able to handle anything thrown at us as long as we remained in God's will. Even though he believed as long as we chose to follow God we would continue to be blessed, when things became difficult he found himself behaving as his father did—meeting anger with anger.

The powerful feeling of being unstoppable began to diminish within months of having Johnny and his sisters in our home. I remembered how I had judged the woman who had returned them to child protective services, but within three months of living with them, I completely understood her decision. Even though I had Bundy, my mom, and a family support system, I was struggling—there was no way a single, retired woman was going to manage them. When their behavioral problems emerged during that first year, and they attended mandatory counseling,

Child Protective Services showed us previous reports of theirs. Reading these reports it became clear Child Protective Services had openly lied when they told us these children had no problems. The reports revealed to us what the children had been through, and as they grew older, they began to disclose more and more of what they had experienced.

We discovered over the ensuing year of fostering the children that raising them wasn't as easy as just applying love and discipline. The three had serious trauma attachment problems, ingrained over years of moving from home to home. We were naïve to believe our training had prepared us to manage the effects of such deep-seated trauma. The training did help a little, especially with providing insight into what we were dealing with, but it was tenacity and the determined choice not to give up that kept us going. Children with reactive attachment disorder are not bad children, the disorder subconsciously tells them they are not worth love; that you don't really love them, and they will prove you can't love them. They show affection and call you mom, then uncaringly hurt you. These three siblings had been returned to child protective services twice before by foster parents who couldn't deal with their behavior.

My mom is the one I went crying to when it became too much for me. She knows her decision to never give up on me in my difficult years motivated my decision to adopt. I wanted to provide that support for children who didn't have a mom to stand up for them. We laugh when I remind my mom of the curse she put on me when I was a rebellious teenager and gave her such a hard time—"I hope your children are just as bad as you, or worse!" We joke now that I received my behavior back tenfold. What I also learned from adopting these siblings was an appreciation for my adoptive dad. I was a very strong-willed child and I butted heads with him continually. I hadn't really had much respect for him until I realized the sacrifice required to adopt a child and raise her to be self-assured, and equipped to face the world.

That first year of Johnny, Cristina, and Kayla being in our home was exceptionally tough. We constantly tried to show them we truly do love them, and did our best to assure them they were now, and always would be, part of a forever family. We quickly realized convincing them of this was not going to be as easy as it was with Nidra and Cory. We expected a close relationship between the three of them, but there wasn't, and they fought constantly. The slightest attempt at discipline caused conflict. When a simple task like washing the dishes was refused, and we were threatened—the threat of calling Child Protective Services and (falsely) reporting abuse was leveled against us—I offered the phone to the child who had made this threat. We allowed them the freedom to complain and protest, but continued to apply the discipline they needed. I admit to times of selfish anger at their lack of appreciation for what we were offering. There appeared to be no gratitude for all they had been given. I understood their reluctance to accept our love after having lived in a number of different homes and having called several women mom, but still; we were offering them real love, in our home, and our family, and they didn't appreciate it.

Johnny, Cristina, and Kayla were removed from their

mother's custody due to her substance abuse and subsequent neglect. These children were taken from the custody of their parents and then given back a number of times. Soon after the last sibling was born, they were taken away for good. In fact, some of the siblings actually tested positive for drugs when they were born. The State was obviously adamant about keeping these children away from their parents after this evidence was revealed. The children's grandmother cared for them whenever their parents lost custody, and the older siblings were apparently raised mostly by their grandmother. When their parents lost custody of the children completely, and the grandmother passed away, the State felt their adult siblings would not cope with the emotional and financial stress of caring for all the children, so the youngest baby was adopted, and Johnny, Cristina, and Kayla were placed in the foster care system.

Once in the foster care system they lived in fifteen different homes over a period of eight years. One can only imagine how damaging this must have been for the siblings. Some believe more damage is done to children in the foster system than they would experience in a family home, even if

neglected. One of our adopted daughters vividly remembers being

sexually abused while in foster care, whereas the other does not.

Many abused children repress bad memories just to survive, but

still suffer the awful consequences. The children were placed in

the foster-to-adopt program in Kentucky, and at some point—in

one of the fifteen different homes they had been placed—the

Department of Child Protective Services found the siblings

locked in dog cages in the backyard. I believe the foster system in

America is a breeding ground for human trafficking.

We knew this situation was bigger than we were. We

would not have chosen to foster three children at once, especially

with two of them being girls. We chose to trust God and accept

He had put these children into our lives as part of His greater

plan. Bundy has a large presence, and although he never lifted his

hand, when he yells, it is most disturbing to everybody. We had to

frequently coax ourselves out of our anger, going over their

history and the trauma they suffered, earnestly trying to

understand their behavior. We wanted to show them a loving

family, how to look out and care for each other. We had to constantly make intentional choices. We chose to love them, even when it hurt. We chose to keep trying, to keep praying, and to go on loving them, even as they pushed us away. We chose not to give up. Most importantly, we chose to accept adoption is forever, just as God has adopted us into His family.

Soon after adopting Johnny and his sisters, Bundy expressed our feelings on adoption in a message he shared with the church. Among the many blessings of the Christian experience is adoption. The New Testament word for adoption means "to place as an adult son,"[3] and has to do with our standing in the family of God. We are the children of God by faith in Christ, born into God's family. God does not regard us as little children, but adult sons and daughters, with all the legal rights and privileges of an heir. When someone chooses to trust Christ and is saved, he is a "spiritual babe"[4] who needs to grow, but as

3 *The Wiersbe Bible Commentary: New Testament*, p. 564, Published by David C. Cook, 4050 Lee Vance View, Colorado Springs, CO 80918 U.S.A. © 2007 Warren W. Wiersbe

4 Ibid p. 564

far as his position is concerned, he is an adult son who can draw on the Father's wealth, and can exercise all the rights of a son. The children we adopted can and should expect to share in the same love, care, and nurturing our biological children do, with the same legal rights in our home and our name. God did not give up on us, even when we were sinners, so we can't give up on our children, no matter what they do.

One thing everyone shared was a love for Reggie, because he was hyper-playful, and loving to everyone. The older kids were often responsible for watching Reggie—doing his therapy homework with him, or just making sure he didn't hurt himself or others by accident. One day, while playing baseball in the living room with the other kids, Reggie swung the plastic bat and broke the big-screen TV set. We were grateful no one was hurt. Something Johnny and Reggie shared was a love for the trampoline, and they would often jump together for hours.

My mom gave me the emotional reassurance I needed, and we received a lot of support from our friends, family, and church members. Being an extrovert, I need and want to process my feelings externally. I have no problem trusting people, and I don't care if they share what I tell them. I feel it's about being able to talk when you need to, and having people to lean on. That's what I did through this entire process, Mom first, then my best friend, and then whoever is trustworthy who would listen. I want to help others too, so it's great if hearing and discussing my experiences does that. When the church became aware we had taken the three siblings in, they came together and provided any additional clothes and furniture we needed. Church members also did the remodeling of our home, so we only had to pay for the supplies rather than hiring a contractor, saving us sixty percent of the remodeling costs.

We made two more attempts at fostering to adopt but neither worked out. The first boy didn't really feel comfortable with our family and asked to be moved, and the second one was older and sort of transitioning into adult life. He already had a job and a car and wasn't looking for a family. Each boy stayed with us for a while then left. After the second one left we realized this is it—we have our family; and we stopped trying to adopt after that, and got on with our lives. My adoptive father's family held an annual reunion in Kentucky, which I enjoyed every year as a girl, but which I hadn't attended since marrying Bundy. Mine was a very white, country family, and although I didn't remember any racist behavior in my youth, I was concerned there may be offensive remarks or behavior toward our family. I wanted to attend the reunion, but we had lived through a difficult year with our recently adopted children, and I didn't want to put them through any more unpleasantness.

While we pondered this decision we were unaware that, as difficult as we may have thought the past year was, it was in fact still part of the honeymoon period of our lives. We had no idea of what was about to happen to our family, and that the honeymoon period was at an end.

Source: © 2018 Francis and Cristi Bundukamara
Order from top left to right:
  Nidra, Bundy, Johnny, Cristi, Cristina, Cory
Order from bottom left to right: Reggie, Kayla, and Miah

Chapter Six: Tragedy Strikes

We had been traveling a long road and when we pulled up at a gas station, I was surprised to see a man come over and ask Bundy how much gas we needed. Yeah, in Stearns, they still have a guy who pumps gas into your tank. Stearns is a tiny town in McCreary County, Kentucky. The guy came up and introduced himself to Bundy, and though I wasn't certain, it seemed like this guy wanted to be friends with him... almost like he had never seen a black person before. It was strange but also encouraging. I mean, this guy actually offered Bundy a Yoohoo™ chocolate drink. It was definitely not what we had expected. Back home in Florida we had been concerned about the possibility of encountering some racism in Kentucky, but we had finally decided to accept my family's invitation to their annual reunion.

Thinking the guy at the gas station had just been a particularly friendly person, we were surprised yet again when we got the same kind of reception in a grocery store. Now, Bundy is the kind of guy who talks to everybody, he does that all the time, but when another total stranger started talking to him in this little town, it went completely against our expectation. When the guy in the grocery store realized that Bundy and I were actually married, people in the store seemed genuinely happy for us. Contrary to our expectation, we had detected no tone of racism at all in this little town. It also seemed most people knew each other because when we said we had come to town for the Ross reunion, they knew exactly who we meant.

We had, for many years, avoided this reunion because we assumed the people in Kentucky were racist, and that something would happen to offend us. I have a distant cousin from Kentucky who was brutally beaten by her black boyfriend, and this is why I initially thought my family was reluctant to accept interracial relationships. Bundy, who doesn't normally prejudge people, was drawn into my concern about experiencing racism. He was obviously not excited about the reunion, which he didn't want to attend. I knew my family would not be overtly prejudiced toward us—we are generally respectful to each other, so my concern was more about the country people we would meet. I thought they might be outwardly offensive to us but as it turned out, my assumptions were unfounded. The friendly people we met at the gas station and the store were defining moments for us. We recognized we had misjudged these people.

My dad grew up in Indiana, but his parents were from this small mining town in Kentucky. His father was a miner, and his family all lived in a mining town. It was very dangerous work but mining was a popular career choice during that era. It was a tight little mining community, and the house my dad lived in is about a mile from the Cumberland River. This is where all the Ross family reunions are held, in this small house situated in the Southfork National Park. I used to go to all the reunions as a kid but this was actually the first time I had gone since being married. My dad's parents had lots of brothers and sisters, who would all come together, so there'd be somewhere between thirty to fifty family members who would come together every year for this reunion. Aunts, uncles, distant cousins—most of them were no longer from Kentucky.

So, every year, people would all arrive for the reunion.

There was space for only a few people inside the small house, others stayed with local relatives or in hotels and cabins. Sometimes, families would set up their campsites in the large field surrounding the house. We set up our home-base for the holiday, and feeling relaxed, we started enjoying the festive vacation atmosphere. We spent time mingling and chatting to our extensive family while we barbecued that first evening, with Bundy and I both feeling relieved at how the day had unfolded. Tired but happy, we slept well, looking forward to a day at the waterhole, where children could paddle in the shallows, and the older children and adults could swim the river or kayak at their leisure.

Early the next morning, we loaded about ten people and a stack of tubes into the back of somebody's pickup truck, and we drove down to the river. I have a cousin named Steven who is always a really prominent figure at the reunion—if ever Steven wasn't able to make it to the reunion, everybody would be upset. Steven and I were really close when we were younger—he's about five years younger than me. We would often go rock climbing, and I remember rappelling down huge waterfalls with him. Steven is always fun to be with, probably because he is so active. Well, on our first day of vacation, Steven took Bundy out on an adventure he will never forget! In typical Steven style, he got Bundy to do two things he would *never* normally do.

He took Bundy hiking in the woods, which was already out of Bundy's comfort zone but then, in the middle of their hike, he told Bundy to look down... Bundy looked down and immediately he froze. He was perched on top of an arch, hundreds of feet above the ground. Bundy was scared to death—he has a fear of heights, and he ended up on his hands and knees, crawling off the arch. This is the type of thing my cousin Steven does, probably to draw people out of their comfort zone, but also to have fun watching their reaction. After their walk in the woods, Steven took Bundy on a four-wheel drive through mud so thick that Bundy came back covered in mud from head to toe—you couldn't even tell he was a black guy. It was Bundy's initiation into our 2005 family reunion.

Bundy and Steven went down to the river to clean up, and Bundy spent the rest of the afternoon keeping an eye on Reggie and Miah, who were splashing in the shallows near the water's edge. Johnny was having a great time swimming in the waterhole with his newfound cousins, a group of teenaged boys roughly his own age. He wasn't a very strong swimmer, so we insisted he wear a lifejacket. Cristina and Kayla were also splashing about in the shallows or sunning themselves on the grassy verge lining the river. The boys were playing boisterous river games in the swimming hole, as teenaged boys will do. The swimming hole was very deep but the water slowed down in this area of the river, and was not affected by the current further out, toward the middle of the river. The river has a history of being very deep, and when I was a child I grew up hearing stories about how endlessly deep the water hole was, and that no one had ever been to the bottom. We were warned to be careful of the dinosaur-sized catfish that lived at the bottom of the swimming hole, but it was all said in fun, as no one had ever gotten hurt at this swimming hole.

We had another great evening socializing with our

74

extended family over the evening meal, and discussed our plans for the next day. Bundy doesn't particularly like swimming. In fact, he has a slight phobia about water. He struggles to float, so even though everybody tells him all he has to do is relax, as soon as he tries relaxing he immediately starts sinking to the bottom. So Bundy decided not to do anything special the next day. He was happy to sit on the porch with Reggie and the girls, just relaxing and enjoying his time out. Johnny was happy to hang out with the other boys, having fun in the swimming hole. I was keen to do something different, so Steven and I arranged to go on a river kayaking adventure. Two other family members chose to join us on our excursion up the river. We would be kayaking along a stretch of the Cumberland River, which is protected by the National Park Service.

I ate breakfast with Bundy and the children before loading the kayak I would be using onto the back of a pickup. I waved to Bundy, who was sitting on the porch with Cristina, Kayla, Reggie, and Miah. A second pickup was being loaded with tubes by a boisterous group of boys, and I saw Johnny among them, laughing and chatting. It was so good to see my boy finally revealing the more bubbly side to his personality, which was usually hidden behind a sometimes painfully shy exterior. I caught Johnny's eye and waved. His face lit up, and he waved back. Then he turned, and placing his hands behind him on the open tailgate, lifted himself onto it with a backward jump. The pickup was now overflowing with excited boys and rubber tubes. I saw Steven's wife and another adult woman—the mother of two boys sitting on the pickup tailgate with Johnny—loading the front of the pickup with food and drinks for a day at the river. They would be supervising the rowdy group of boys. Steven's wife waved to us as we headed down the dirt track toward the river.

It was a beautiful day, and I was at peace with my world as I drove down to the river with my kayaking companions. I was glad we had decided to attend this year's family reunion. Steven, who lives in the area, knows this section of the river intimately, having spent most of his life hiking, swimming, and kayaking the South Fork of the Cumberland River. The early morning sunlight struck the river and was deflected into the trees on the opposite bank, creating a wash of sparkling light on the canopy of leaves. Steven saw me appreciating the beauty of the scene before us and he grinned knowingly. "We've missed you at our reunions these past years, Cristi. It's good to have you and your family here with us," he said, lifting a red and white kayak off the pickup and handing it to me.

"It's good to be here, Steven," I replied sincerely, placing my kayak into the water. The four of us settled into our shallow seats, then pushed off from the bank with our paddles.

Our paddles splashed softly in the water as we guided our kayaks into the current and began working our way upstream. Surrounded by the beauty of nature I relished the feel of my muscles working, and my mind drifted freely, resting briefly on how blessed my life was. I had married a really good man who loved me, I had seven beautiful children, and we lived in our dream home. It felt like my honeymoon had never ended. The sun was higher in the sky when I first heard the growl of an engine. A few minutes later, we saw a park ranger standing on a large rock on the bank, and he called out to us, telling us to get off the river. Steven was frowning, and when I caught his eye he said, "Something's wrong. They don't do this." We paddled over to where the ranger stood but even though we called out to him, asking why he wanted us off the river, he would not say why they had stopped us. "Our family is down-river, what's going on?" shouted Steven. The ranger said he didn't really know. We were probably about a mile or two from the swimming hole, and Steven immediately broke into a run.

We all had a sense of foreboding, knowing something was wrong. Steven had called out to us to wait, and that he would send somebody back for us in a pickup. My uncle, Alenn, came back for us in a pickup, and while we made our way back to the swimming hole, he told me Johnny had gone missing. He had apparently tried to swim across the river with the other boys but started struggling, and he went under before anyone could get close enough to help. My heart was beating fast, and all I could think of was, *I've got to get the girls! Surely Johnny would have worn his lifejacket before deciding to follow the other boys across the river?*

When we arrived, I walked down to the bank to see what was happening. There were rescue divers in the water and paramedics on the bank. The divers hadn't found Johnny yet, and I just stood on the bank in shock. Bundy joined me on the bank, along with the girls. I held Cristina and Kayla, and we just stood there, crying. Steven was still diving, frantically searching for Johnny in the bottomless depths of the swimming hole. He had been diving from the time he arrived. I found out later when Steven first arrived on the scene, none of the officials even had divers in the water yet. He was the only one in the water, diving, and desperately trying to find Johnny. Stories of how deep the river was in this area crowded my mind. Stories about this section of the river being an endless hole, and that no one had ever been to the bottom.

Bundy knew it wasn't a good situation but even at this seemingly hopeless moment, he kept praying. He knew prayer could move mountains, so he was praying for the divers to find

Johnny. There is a rock on the riverbank, about twenty feet high, that the boys would use to launch themselves into the water, so we knew the waterhole was really deep. I stared into the light-brown river water, desperately trying to see through the murky depths in the hope of sighting Johnny. Try as I might, I couldn't see through it, and I knew Steven and the other divers were facing a very difficult task. I remember standing on the edge of the bank holding Cristina and Kayla, with Bundy praying feverishly for the divers to find Johnny.

Johnny had disappeared underwater at least twenty minutes before I had arrived, and as a nurse, I knew the time that had passed really limited Johnny's chance of survival. There seemed to be no hope. I began to think about how we could help the girls... after all they had already been through, this just seemed to be terribly unfair. I had promised them they would be safe, not knowing at the time how quickly tragedy can strike a family.

Many hours later one of the divers finally found Johnny. It

took them what felt like a really long time to find his body. I stood on the edge of the riverbank feeling utter shock and disbelief that God had allowed this. Mostly, I was shocked that God would allow this to happen to Cristina and Kayla, especially after all they had been through. Bundy was also in a state of shock. He had reached a point in his life where he honestly thought everything was going to be all right, so what happened to Johnny really jolted him. It came like a bolt from the blue. When I recently asked him how he tanding on the riverbank after Johnny's lifeless body had been found, he couldn't remember his feelings. The only thing he remembers feeling is how unfair it was that this had happened to us.

Within a couple hours of finding Johnny's body, we were on the road home. All I wanted was my mom. Heading south, we drove back to Florida straight through the night, and my uncle, whose house is about four hours north of ours, was following us home. On the drive home we struggled to get hold of Cory. Because he was in basic training we had to call through the Red Cross—you can't just call someone who is in basic training. I remember talking to Cory and telling him about what had happened, and then I called a few other friends, but all I really wanted was just to be home. Once my uncle had reached his house, we continued driving the final stretch to our home alone.

I was driving, and I remember being pulled over by the police for speeding. I probably looked like a battered wife, having been up all night and crying my eyes out. The policeman asked me to get out of the car, and took me to the back of the vehicle because I was obviously upset. He could see all the kids in the back, and he asked me if I was all right, maybe thinking I was being bullied by Bundy. I told him my son had just died, and then I fell to the ground, sobbing and feeling on the verge of hysteria. The policeman told Bundy to get out of the car—I don't know how long we stopped for—maybe twenty or thirty minutes, and then he told Bundy to take over the driving.

It was a really awful time in our lives. It shattered Cristina and Kayla's trust in our ability to care for them, and Bundy and I began to wonder where we had gone wrong. Of course, over time, we realized that some things are simply beyond our control, but in that moment we had to dig deep to stay connected to God. After Johnny died, some other things happened, and Bundy experienced a really difficult time over that following year. He was angry, and went through a time of not liking the Lord. He was going to seminary, and was just trying to carry on with his life but he wasn't happy at all. Even though Bundy was upset, and still trying to process what had happened to Johnny, he was surprised to realize that he still loved Jesus.

When we try to find meaning in Johnny's death, it becomes clear to us that God used Johnny to bring Cristina and Kayla into our lives—there's no doubt in our minds. We had absolutely no intention of adopting more girls—no intention at all! It saddens me that we had no time to develop a deep relationship with Johnny. He was such a shy boy, and he was just coming out of his shell. I mean, this was the first time we had seen him running around happy. He had been happy at other times too, like at school with his friends, but this was the first time Johnny came out of his shell during a family event. Although

Johnny was distant, and did not fight outwardly for his sisters, he had taken on the role of protecting them. Johnny never caused any drama, and had a somewhat timid personality.

He also wasn't a very touchy-feely kind of person, and we actually had to intervene at one point between Johnny and Cristina. Cristina definitely *does* have a touchy-feely personality—if you know anything about love languages—she needs a hug every day! The problem came about when she wanted to hug Johnny every day, all the time, and she would really get into his personal space. Johnny didn't like it, so we had to make a rule that Johnny hug Cristina once a day, and then Cristina had to leave him alone and not touch him the rest of the day. This story still makes us smile now but at the time we had to treat it seriously. We often tell this story and laugh about it to this day. Johnny's death was a huge loss for us, but it was a million times more of a loss for the girls. His death had a devastating effect on Cristina and Kayla. It was easier for me to stay strong— I didn't know why God had allowed this to happen, and I knew I would be okay—but I also knew this was going to have a way bigger effect on Johnny's two sisters. They had no way of making sense of this tragedy. There is, however, one positive thing that happened in Johnny's life that brings us some peace of mind.

Johnny had first started coming out of his shell when he went on a church camp. We knew we had told Johnny about Christ but we weren't sure yet if he had developed a personal relationship with Him. We really didn't know because, like I said, he was so shy he wouldn't openly have these conversations with us. It isn't as if he was walking around the house cussing, and he wouldn't openly deny Christ either, but there was no real way for us to know what was going on inside his head and in his heart. We thought we would have more time to share the gospel in his life.

After hearing about Johnny's death, the youth leader remembered an activity they did at camp. The activity was to write a letter to God, so she fervently went through all the camp letters, found Johnny's, and immediately came to our home. The letter was simple and sweet, just like Johnny's personality: "God help me to be a better Christian, and be closer to God." This letter blessed us immensely, and we gladly hold on to the truth that our son had accepted Jesus as his Lord. Although Johnny's death marks the beginning of a very difficult time, we chose to continue following God. We also chose to acknowledge that we really did love Johnny very much and that his death had hurt our hearts, and sadly, that his death had begun to chip away at our blind faith in God...

Source: © 2018 Francis and Cristi Bundukamara
Johnny, Cory and Reggie

Chapter Seven: Seizures Hit Hard

Reggie's laughter rose above the noise of the family gathering. I could hear him laughing from the kitchen where I was chatting and catching up with the other women. There were kids everywhere, running around boisterously, with everyone excited to see each other. I heard Reggie stop laughing, and continued chatting until I was jolted by hearing my name screamed in panic.

With all her children grown and enjoying Christmas at their own homes each year, my mother had introduced a tradition of holding a family breakfast at her home on Christmas Eve. Our family is a large one, and my mom's new husband's family is just as big, so there were lots of people at their home that day. Everyone was having a good time eating together, spending time with family, and playing with the kids. My brother, Wayne, was playing with the children by spinning them around. He held both their hands and, starting slowly, spun them around until their feet lifted off the floor. Being a sensory seeker, it was a game Reggie especially enjoyed.

We rushed to the source of the scream, and running outside, I saw Reggie on the floor in the throes of a grand mal seizure. Convulsing, foaming at the mouth, every muscle in his body rigid... I hurried over, and kneeling next to him, turned him onto his side. My training and experience told me what this was, and what I should do, but no amount of practical knowledge prepares you emotionally for seeing your child experience his first grand mal seizure. I suppressed my alarm and called for a cushion to put under Reggie's head, told someone to call 911, and held Reggie on his side. The ambulance and rescue workers arrived pretty quickly, but the seizure had ended by then. I freeze emotionally in a crisis situation, and my brain processes the information it receives from all angles. I recognized the magnitude of what this meant. This wasn't going to be the only seizure Reggie would have. It was confirmation there was definitely something bigger going on with Reggie.

The rescue workers took Reggie to Baptist Hospital where they monitored him and ran some tests, but the seizure had passed and there was not much else they could do. The excitement, and being swung around probably brought on the seizure, but it would have happened at some point anyway. Normally, they would have kept Reggie overnight at least, but with my experience as a nurse, and it being Christmas Eve, they allowed us to go home to celebrate Christmas. But Christmas would never be the same again.

Although Reggie had been diagnosed with ADHD, the first sign we were dealing with something more was when he was diagnosed with dyspraxia in May, 2006. As it turned out, that particular diagnosis wasn't significant, as dyspraxia is a blanket term for difficulty controlling movement or speech. The doctors were trying to figure out what was happening with Reggie, and autism, another umbrella term, was later also diagnosed. Reggie had been having difficulty since he was quite young, which is characteristic of autism, except autistic children typically have social difficulties and Reggie was the opposite, he had always been extremely social.

After Reggie had the grand mal seizure on Christmas Eve,

I was in a state of shock for some time after. It made all my work trying to fix Reggie's condition seem worthless. It made clear to us his learning problems were far bigger than we believed, and he was much sicker than we understood. Around the same time, Miah started having difficulty maintaining the academic standard at the advanced school she was in, so we transferred her to a regular school. We made the choice to keep learning, to keep going and never give up. We chose to continue fighting.

Kayla has always been a strong-willed individual. As a child she was also very oppositional, and we saw some of her more negative character traits start escalating after Johnny's death. Bundy and I were distraught at Johnny's death, but Cristina and Kayla didn't possess the emotional tools to deal with their loss. Bundy and I relied on each other to keep our family strong and positive, but Cristina and Kayla, with their limited life experience, were unable to make sense of the world after Johnny's death. The only real choice we could make was to continue loving our daughters; but even then, I think we used too much "tough love." There was a fairly widespread church movement regarding discipline and tough love at that time, and we thought the best approach would be to stay consistent in how we disciplined negative behavior. Tough love requires positive reinforcement though, and I believe this is where we fell short.

When I say Kayla's oppositional behavior began escalating after Johnny's death, we noticed how certain character traits became more pronounced. She had previously exaggerated facts, but now she began saying things that stretched the truth. We also noticed that while Kayla had been emotionally distant before Johnny's death, she had now become hard-hearted. Of course, this was a fairly natural response to the trauma she experienced with her brother's death, especially given the extreme hardship she and her siblings had been through in their lives.

Cory enjoyed making people laugh, and was well liked because he was fun to be around. He did also tend to avoid difficult situations and issues. We were pleased when he volunteered to join the military reserve force while still a junior in high school. He completed the basic training between his junior and senior year, and before graduating high school he went on an eight week training course with the coast guard in Miami. He was committed to military duty one weekend a month, but he ceased to report for duty soon after graduating. It turned out that it wasn't what he really wanted, and had only joined to make us proud of him. He did not complete his enlistment and was eventually admin discharged. Cory began to adopt a laissez-faire approach to life. He later met a girl, moved in with her and disappeared from our lives for about two years. Bundy was a little disappointed, but felt we had done what we could for him, and because he was a man now, he was making his own choices. His disappearance, especially when I discovered he had been living with his biological mom for a while, hurt me. I could feel the tears forming as I wondered if he still loved me. It was a feeling of sadness and betrayal, followed by an understanding that if I was in his position I would also want a relationship with my mom. Then I thought, *She didn't make the effort to keep him, and now that he's an adult she wants to resurrect the relationship.* This was, of course, followed by the guilt of judging her. All I wanted was a relationship with my son.

As mentioned earlier, I know when something is bothering one of my children, and during Nidra's training at Job Corps, when she met Tallant, I could see she had something significant on her mind. I devised a situation where Nidra and I could be alone and then said to her, "I know you have something to tell me." After some hesitation, Nidra breathed deeply and told me she was pregnant with Tallant's baby. My mind raced back to when I was sixteen year's old and pregnant. Fear of being ill equipped to deal with a baby, sadness at the loss of my youth, anxiety about the future, and the uncertainty of not knowing what to do about any of it flashed through my mind. During my teenage pregnancy, my mother and grandmother had offered to pay for an abortion, and we simply made the decision without much thought. An abortion was arranged. As I looked at my daughter I had a sense of the difficulties that lay ahead of her—the challenges facing a young, single mother—and I began to understand my own mother's concern for me when she offered that choice on my behalf. Looking back to when I was sixteen, I don't remember discussing other options. I never even considered I was carrying a living child. Little did I know, guilty thoughts about my own selfishness would plague me for years to come.

I felt protective of Nidra, and didn't want her burdened with the responsibility of a child before she had firmly established the course of her life. As Christians, abortion wasn't a route we would go, so we listed the options, and I recommended Nidra give the baby up for adoption. Her determination and self-assurance were made clear when she refused to give up her baby, but because she was an adopted child, what she told me made me sad. She told me she felt that adoption was worse than abortion. When I saw the depth of Nidra's emotional attachment to her unborn baby, I regretted suggesting adoption to her.

I suggested adoption without considering the love a mother has for her child. For someone who had a biological mother who she felt didn't love her, suggesting she give her child up was the worst thing I could have said. One thing I tell young mothers looking for advice is, "You do what you think is best at the time, but you may be wrong." I feel terribly guilty about suggesting Nidra give her child up. I still look back at it today and say to myself, "Gosh that was wrong!" I still beat myself up about the emotional rift it caused between us for a while, but Nidra seems to be over it. A part of me, however, was pleased, because it showed she had the emotional resolve to make her own judgment. Bundy had always been Nidra's role model, even before she became part of our family. They have a great relationship and are very close, but when we told Bundy Nidra was pregnant, we kept from him the fact that the baby's father was married. Believing in Nidra, Bundy trusted the decision she would make, and didn't try to urge her in any direction.

During this time it seemed to me Bundy was mindful of what was going on with the rest of the family but he wasn't really paying attention to what was going on with Reggie. I later realized he was just scared and confused. He had always compared his faith to Abraham's, and felt he should leave everything in the Lord's hands. After Johnny's death, however, and being forced to recognize Reggie was having problems,

Bundy was having a hard time. He was struggling through finding

how best to deal with it all, because when Bundy's family hurts,

he hurts. I went into fix-it mode and began researching how to

treat every diagnosis Reggie was given. We tried one herbal

product, then a supplement, which led us into alternative

medication. Each alternative doctor has their own method of

treatment, and they prescribed loads of supplements, costing us

thousands of dollars. We did it over and over with each new

diagnosis. When they said autism, we went into autism

treatments—hyperbaric oxygen and specific diets, gluten free,

casein free, and so on. Although, once we started with improved

nutrition, we kept it up.

In August of 2006, Savanna made her grand entrance into

our family. Unfortunately she chose to arrive twelve weeks early,

and was born weighing a mere two pounds and eight ounces. She

was put on a ventilator to assist her tiny lungs, and spent the

beginning of her life in the neonatal intensive care unit. Nidra was

a pillar of courage and resilience as Savanna struggled to flourish

for the first few years of her life. Anxiety levels peaked when the doctors informed us she would need surgery on her underdeveloped little heart. The date for surgery was set for October 5th, 2007. Tallant, Savanna's father, really rose to the occasion. He supported Nidra in every way, caring for both Nidra and Savanna throughout that stressful and volatile time. We tried to support Nidra and be as much help as we could, but she was independent now, living on her own, and quite honestly, we were wrapped up with other issues in our family. Savanna's heart surgery was a success, to everyone's enormous relief. We were so proud of Nidra, and how she stayed strong during that tense and critical period. Seeing her with Savanna now, I again deeply regret suggesting Nidra give her up.

In 2007, Reggie started chelation therapy, and heavy metals, specifically arsenic, were emerging from his body. We investigated the possible sources of arsenic he may have been exposed to during his early childhood, and also on our current property, trying to locate any area that could potentially have contributed to his problems. We even asked the school he attended to test for arsenic. By 2008, Reggie's seizures had become uncontrollable, and were increasing in frequency and intensity. We went to New York University (NYU) Epilepsy center next, where they diagnosed Reggie with Lennox-Gastaut Syndrome (LGS.) At that point I was angry with the diagnosis, knowing LGS was another "bucket" diagnosis, so we refused to accept this new diagnosis, and we returned to our Miami doctors to get their opinions.

By this stage we had become frustrated with the medical community. Bundy had been hopeful we would get some answers from the NYU Epilepsy Center; after all, they were supposed to be the best. We kept receiving different diagnoses for Reggie but many seemed incorrect, and none of them made sense. Reggie's seizure and developmental presentation was very different from other children with the same symptoms. We sensed some doctors were clearly guessing, with diagnoses like autism, LGS, and mental retardation. One doctor even said, "Some kids are just mentally retarded and have seizures." We knew Reggie had been born completely normal and had been deteriorating over time. Even his IQ was decreasing. The many hospital visits meshed in my mind. There were two distinct periods—the early diagnosis period at Miami Children's Hospital where we were hopeful, and the later period where everyone seemed so negative we just wanted to get out of there.

Bundy chose to ignore the bad news, and together we chose to not believe the skepticism. We chose to continue looking for hopeful doctors, and we continued to love on Reggie and do our best to help him. One of the best choices we made was to go back to our Miami doctors with this supposedly new diagnosis to see what they had to say about it. They strongly disagreed with the diagnosis of Lennox-Gastaut Syndrome, and continued assessing Reggie. This contrary diagnosis had ultimately provided them with renewed motivation to find the cause of Reggie's illness.

Source: © 2018 Francis and Cristi Bundukamara
Cristina, Kayla, Reggie and Miah

Chapter Eight: PTSD Almost Ruined Us

"This man abuses me!" said Kayla to the emergency room nurse, after Bundy had left the room for a soda. When he returned, he was taken into a private room with two security guards and told what Kayla had said. In a few short seconds, his anger level was right back up to where it had been an hour earlier, when he had wrestled Kayla off me... but Kayla didn't stop there. "He broke my foot because he lost his temper, and this isn't the first time he's physically abused me!" Still reeling from her false accusations, it suddenly struck Bundy that nobody here knew the truth—the two hospital security guards probably helped him with this realization, as they looked on him what seemed to be judgment. Bundy was told the police would arrive shortly to question him. As the guards turned their backs and closed the door, he heard the click of a lock, and couldn't believe what was unfolding. As the shock of what had just happened began to wear off, Bundy's anger once more began to steadily rise. As enraged as he was, another emotion dwarfed his anger: his heart was aching with the sharp pain of his daughter's betrayal.

The police arrived, and Bundy was thoroughly interrogated. After answering some harsh questions about the alleged child abuse, the police withdrew from the room. Bundy expressed "It's a strange feeling, knowing your own innocence, yet somehow feeling a sense of shame and guilt. I suppose it was simply the thought of these strangers—who didn't know my heart, and possibly did not believe me—thinking I might actually abuse my own children. It was a terrible ordeal to go through, one I hope never to experience again!"

Even as Bundy sat there with his head in his hands, feeling betrayed and outraged, the ordeal was not yet over. As soon as the police had withdrawn, an official from Child Protective Services entered the room next, to continue the interrogation. This was a pivotal event in his relationship with Kayla, and Bundy had a really hard time trusting her again.

Given their history, it was little wonder that Kayla began showing signs of bad behavior after Johnny's death. Her behavior gradually deteriorated over the next three years. At that stage we didn't really realize how bad it was or how bad it was going to get. We just thought her behavior was exaggerated teenage stuff. In May of 2008, we gave Kayla her first cell phone for her fourteenth birthday. That was the day we lost control. Before long, we found sex texts and explicit pictures on her phone, and when confronted she didn't respond well. Shortly afterward, Kayla ran away from home with a boy who lived in a house with no rules, and spent a lot of time hanging out on the street.

Nidra was able to find Kayla, and managed to trick her into being outside at a specific time. Nidra and Cory went into the ghetto area where Kayla was living and aggressively picked her up. Nidra was so angry with what Kayla was doing to the family, she grabbed her and threw her into the car, threatening to punch her in the face. To our dismay, Kayla ran away again and again... it was impossible to keep her off the streets. After lots of searching for an affordable teen program, we sent her to Teen Challenge Kansas City Girls Home in 2009. Teen Challenge is a fifteen-month residential discipleship program based on establishing a relationship with Jesus Christ, and is geared toward positive life transformation and restoring relationships. Once the Teen challenge program had accepted Kayla, Bundy and I breathed a collective sigh of relief. Kayla was now safe and off the streets, and hopefully on the way to learning how to deal with her childhood mistreatment. We also hoped the program would help Kayla to overcome her reactive attachment issues. We could now focus on sourcing doctors and treatment for Reggie. This relief was short lived, as we had no idea what Cristina had in store for us.

At the same time, Cristina was going through her own crisis, which meant another crisis for Bundy and I. Speaking to Cristina as an adult, she gave me some perspective on what she had been going through. She told me everything started falling apart when Johnny died. Then Reggie got sick, and started having seizures, which really terrified her. She felt empty and didn't think there was any reason to live, so she decided it would be easier just to run away. For some reason her main goal was to stay away from home longer than Kayla did. I suppose with Johnny's death and Kayla away, Cristina felt isolated, even though Bundy and I loved her and did our best to encourage her. Although Cristina's behavior was similar to Kayla's—in that they both ran away from home—Cristina's heart was more prone to depression. She is a sensitive soul, and just wanted to escape all the hardship she had endured.

The first time a child runs away from home the police actually look for them. The second time you report a runaway child, however, they're considered a chronic runaway, and are simply listed as missing—the police don't even bother looking for them. So, the first time Kayla ran away we actually had about twenty cops and even a helicopter looking for her, but after that... it's done! They don't do it again. At that point your hands are tied—you just start calling people you know, hoping your child stays connected to some positive friends you can contact; friends who can give you some hints and clues as to their whereabouts. Kayla usually ran away to the low-income neighborhood nearby, and so did Cristina the first time she ran. Nidra knew people in the community, she had friends there, and Bundy also had contacts from working in a school, so they both started putting feelers out.

"Hey guys, Cristina ran away, here's a picture. Tell me if you see her in the neighborhood." Bundy would show these pictures to all his football players. A couple of leads came from Bundy's students.

They would say to him, "Hey, I saw your daughter over at this party," or wherever they had seen her.

Once we found Cristina we felt Teen Challenge would also be the best place for her to learn the spiritual and emotional life skills she so desperately needed. The sense of relief we felt when Cristina went to Teen Challenge was because we could now focus our attention on Reggie and his treatment again.

In fact, Cristina and Kayla were at Teen Challenge treatment center at the same time—Kansas City was the only one that would accept them. We allowed Cristina to return home early, after only ten months, because they were not able to service her learning disability. She was doing really well in the program but academically, she started falling behind. Despite these early difficulties, Cristina did finally complete the program. Unfortunately, Kayla didn't complete the program. She got kicked out for having inappropriate relationships. Looking back on our decision to send the girls away, we recognize that although we thought this was the right thing to do at the time, it may have been a mistake—sending children away who already have attachment issues wasn't good for our relationship. I don't think it helped Kayla at all, and she now refers to it as the "Jesus jail."

When Kayla came home after being expelled from Teen Challenge, we put her in a small private school, and for a few months it seemed like she was doing well. Then we heard she was again involved in an increasingly ungodly relationship, and in December they ran away together. This time we did not go looking for her. We just prayed for her safety, and for her to come home. On Christmas Eve, Kayla returned home, flaunting her inappropriate relationship. She actually expected us to accept this relationship—and her behavior—simply because she had come home of her own accord.

The fact that she purposefully arrived on Christmas Eve also played into her need for drama and to be the center of attention. I answered the door and when I realized what was happening, I suggested Bundy go to our room. I allowed Kayla to come inside but I refused to let the friend into my home. The friend immediately started causing a scene in our front yard, so I called the police. Despite only being fifteen years old, Kayla was trying to talk to me logically, as if *she* was the mature adult, and I simply needed to accept her decision. When she realized I wasn't about to listen to her nonsense, she tried to leave again. The police had not yet arrived, so I grabbed Kayla's arm to prevent her from leaving, but she went ballistic and started attacking me. I tried to get away but Kayla just kept punching and kicking me. At this point Bundy came out of the room and intervened. He grabbed Kayla, using a restraining technique he had learned during his employment in juvenile jail. Kayla fought back so hard she somehow managed to break her foot.

The police arrived, successfully de-escalating the situation, leaving us to take Kayla to the emergency room to see to her broken foot. We couldn't both go to the emergency room because that would mean leaving Reggie alone, so Bundy took Kayla. As explained at the start of this chapter, Kayla made a huge scene at the hospital, and tried to get him arrested. Thankfully, the social worker who came to the hospital to investigate our case was familiar with Kayla and the problems we were having with her—she had been to our home several times. I think she could see the relief on Bundy's face when she walked in because, unlike the policemen, she had a better understanding of who Bundy is. No charges were filed, and Kayla went away to cool off for a while.

It definitely was a pivotal moment for Bundy, and he certainly did have a really hard time trusting Kayla after this incident. Accusing Bundy of abuse was undoubtedly Kayla's worst moment. I commend him for continuing to provide for her even to this day. After Kayla had spent some time away, she came home, but within a week she was in trouble again. In January of 2010 Kayla was approved for a four month treatment program, and I really do believe this program helped Kayla. Although there continued to be many minor incidents after Kayla came home, we

were very proud of her when she graduated high school in 2011.

Source: © 2018 Francis and Cristi Bundukamara
Cristi, Kayla, Miah

Chapter Nine: Devastating Diagnosis

It was a day where you never forget where you were or how you felt. It was one of those days when I decided to work, because I wasn't concerned about this follow-up appointment and I was sure the tests would be normal.

During a previous hospital visit, one of the doctors said she noticed Reggie walked in a way which could indicate the possibility of a genetic disorder in the ataxia family, and told me she would like to perform more genetic testing. I doubted her assessment and I told her it was just during the post-ictal stage after a bad day of seizures, but she said she would like to do the tests anyway. I could see no harm in it, so when the follow-up visit to give feedback for the tests was scheduled I asked Bundy to take Reggie by himself.

I usually attended doctor's visits and handled all the medical stuff in the household, but this day I needed to be in the office, so I was at work the day I received the call that would change our lives. I listened to the geneticist after Bundy handed her the phone to explain to me what he didn't fully understand, his hands full trying to prevent a hyperactive Reggie from tearing up the doctor's office. I went cold as she began to speak, but typed the words into an internet search engine as she spelled them out for me.

Dentatorubral-pallidoluysian atrophy (DRPLA). My heart broke with a sob as she explained what this meant, while the words blurred on the screen in front of me. I lay on the floor of my office crying uncontrollably as each word the doctor spoke shattered my world into smaller and smaller pieces. My affectionate, lively little boy had DRPLA. No words can begin to express the depth of grief at hearing my son would lose his mental ability, experience bone-rattling seizures, and great pain. As if this torment wasn't enough, the first thing I saw after typing in the difficult to pronounce, rare, mental degenerative disorder, were the words: *autosomal dominant*. Most people wouldn't know what this means, but as a nurse practitioner I understood all too clearly what the words on the screen told me. This disorder was given to Reggie either by Bundy or me, and that our daughter, Miah, would also need to be tested for it.

When I hung up the phone my nursing professor colleagues were surrounding me, reading the description silently on the computer screen. No one had to say a word; we all knew the magnitude. They let me just cry and cry, allowing me to express my fear and anger. They held me, hugged me, and were just present in my pain. They organized the cancellation of my classes and made sure I made it home safely. I, completely crushed in spirit, greeted Bundy as he arrived home from the appointment. I attempted to explain DRPLA to Bundy just as the doctor did, but he didn't seem to fully understand.

Over the next few days, my mind raced around the information, considering it from every angle, the magnitude of this diagnosis continued to hit me like a semi-truck. I knew it wasn't just Reggie who was sick—this was much bigger than we had initially thought it was. The shock was devastating, and though it became more difficult to stay positive, we chose not to give up on Reggie's treatment. We chose not to change our mindset just because we had been given a name for this illness. I chose to do rigorous, in-depth research into what we were fighting, and Bundy chose to let me lead the fight with my medical experience.

I was still processing and grieving over the diagnosis, and it was time to attend Reggie's annual school IEP meeting. IEP stands for Individualized Education Plan, and in a utopian world it is the plan to successfully teach special needs children. Most special needs parents will tell you it's no utopia and is often stressful. IEP meetings we attended for Reggie were always stressful, as it seemed each meeting focused on what Reggie couldn't do. I always felt the school staff was trying to crush my hope. Reggie started in a regular special education class at a regular elementary school, then was placed in a special program, eventually being transferred to a special handicapped school. I remember leaving each IEP meeting crying. My daily fight was to help Reggie improve, but these meetings were always about how badly he was doing, and that I should reduce my expectations. Every meeting and encounter with schools was a hope killer. I had to go and face these people, and openly admit to having received this horrible diagnosis. I also knew it would be used as justification for why he wasn't teachable.

After Reggie's diagnosis, Bundy, Miah, and I all went for genetic testing. From a few oddities I had noticed in Bundy's movements I suspected he would be positive, but I was certain Miah was healthy. There is a fifty percent chance of not passing the disorder on to a child, and Miah had experienced none of the symptoms Reggie had. When the results of the family genetic testing came back, Bundy had sixty-two repeats, and Miah had sixty-nine! It was another emotionally crushing blow, like a punch to the stomach. As a nurse, having already researched this disorder, I knew that according to the medical community there was little hope.

We were at a loss. How was this possible? They were both so healthy. Miah was having some learning problems, but they seemed so minor compared to what was going on with Reggie. Bundy went into denial. He coached football, he taught high school; he was the king of the castle. When he was at the high school, nothing could touch him. Bundy firmly believed that even when bad things came around, Jesus was with us and in control. We chose hope, thinking that maybe they would never get sick. So little is known about DRPLA. Maybe there was or would be a cure...

Miah was eight years old when we received the diagnosis, so we couldn't tell her about it. I knew it also meant Miah shouldn't have children when she is grown because not only would the fifty percent chance of passing it on to them be a reality, but it also gets worse with each generation. Both our children were so filled with life that the thought of them having DRPLA was gut-wrenching. It took all our emotional strength to fight the grief, and this is when negative thoughts began creeping into my mind. We had to make the conscious decision once again to keep fighting this disorder threatening our family. It was a very difficult time. Reggie's seizures were so devastating and time consuming we didn't even have the emotional energy to process the reality of Miah's diagnosis. Especially since she wasn't sick at that stage. We fervently hoped Miah—like Bundy—would only be affected by adult onset of DRPLA.

Reggie's Disney Cruise- I heard the "ting" as the glass elevator we were packed into reached our floor and the doors opened. We filed out and ambled over to the dining room, looking forward to a nice dinner after the exciting day we had shared. Reaching the dining area I looked around and asked "Where's Reggie?" Panic gripped me as I realized he wasn't with us. We sprinted back to the elevator, but he wasn't there either. Frantic, I stopped the first person I saw who worked for the cruise and told him we had lost our son. He calmly said, "Oh don't worry, kids get lost all the time. It's not a big deal."

"No, you don't understand!" I explained earnestly, "Reggie could jump off the side thinking it's a big swimming pool, it *is* a big deal!" He smiled and told me again not to worry.

"Let's just go to Guest Services, he'll be there." We hurried to the Guest Services desk and asked about Reggie. "No, nobody's brought him yet, but don't worry…"

"You need to make an announcement!" I interrupted, "The kid

doesn't understand he's on a huge boat."

"Oh, we can't make an announcement like that," he told us, "We don't want to scare the other guests."

In 2009 the Make a Wish Foundation had granted Reggie a five day long Disney cruise, and we were able to take Cristina and Kayla along with us. It was so exciting for Reggie because he loved the Disney characters, the water slides and the swimming; everything about the cruise. He was ten years old, but was like a four-year-old who wouldn't wait in line. He would go to the front, give the person a hug, and then step in front of them. Everyone knew we were there on Make a Wish so they tolerated his behavior with a smile. It was good family time with Cristina and Kayla too, as we chose to ignore what they had put us through in the last while, and focused on bonding with them and enjoying the time together.

We have pictures of Reggie playing ping-pong on the cruise, which takes a lot of co-ordination, but his favorite was the big water slide—he would literally spend hours sliding on it. We stopped in the Bahamas and Reggie swam with the dolphins there. It was funny because swimming with the dolphins in the Bahamas was nothing like swimming with the dolphins in Florida. We had swam with the dolphins in Florida several times where the trainers control the dolphins. In the Bahamas they had no control over the dolphins. They told us, "You can't control these animals; they'll come when they want to." It was comical because we knew better, but Reggie loved it, and he laughed and laughed.

He had a really great time on the cruise; it was just the seizures that pretty much knocked him out. At that time Reggie was having seizures in a predictable pattern, two good days then one bad day. He was really tired between seizures but could still do things, so we took him down to the pool and hung out there, or to the children's area where he could play. This is where we eventually found him when he got lost on the way to dinner. Someone had brought him down to the children's area instead of taking him to Guest Services, but he was fine, and was never in any danger. It was one of the longest half hours of my life though.

Source: © 2018 Francis and Cristi Bundukamara
Reggie

Chapter Ten: Cristina and the CRIPs

How could my sweetest daughter get wrapped up in such evil? How, as her mother, did I let this happen? I can only imagine how it happened; even as Cristina tells the story to me, she's emotionally detached. Cristina watched, as if from a far-off distance, as the homemade branding iron was turned slowly over the flame. The emblem being heated was two symbols reflected in one image. When the metal was hot enough for branding, Cristina was told to expose the top of her left thigh. She watched from that place in the distance as the red-hot branding iron was brought into contact with her flesh. A bright surge of pain brought her back into her body, temporarily overriding the sensation-dulling effect of the tranquilizers she had been swallowing like candy. The pain, although reduced, still had the effect of bringing Cristina to a stark realization... she was now a member of the infamous CRIPs!

As someone poured neat whiskey over the burn, Cristina looked at her blistered skin, wondering why it didn't hurt more. Whiskey, Xanax, and marijuana turned what should have been searing pain into mild discomfort. Although Cristina does suffer from anxiety attacks, the pills had not been prescribed by a doctor. There is never a shortage of drugs when one chooses to hang with the CRIPs. This crazy journey started when Cristina was just fifteen—she had first run away from home in 2009, shortly after Kayla was sent to Teen Challenge. She had left to be with a guy who was three years older, but it wasn't long before she was pulled over in a nearby neighborhood by the police. When they ran her name the search revealed she was a missing person, so the mandatory call to her parents was made.

Not knowing how to keep her safe, we decided to send Cristina to Teen Challenge as well. Cristina seemed to do really well emotionally and spiritually during the program. We felt it was the right decision to allow her to come home after only ten months, as they were unable to service her learning disability. Cristina has a normal IQ but has to work harder than most to achieve the same result. When she came home she decided to run away a second time... but this time she ended up running into some deep trouble.

Cristina got wise to our method of tracking her down, and the second time she ran away she went to the Florida Keys. Once she reached the Keys we had lost her, and she knew this. So, it was actually easier to find Kayla, because she would go to neighborhoods where Bundy knew a lot of people. This is why Cristina ended up in the Keys, knowing we didn't have any connections there. Just to reach the Keys from where we lived was about a forty-minute drive, and then another three hours to drive to the furthest point. Cristina took advantage of this the second time she ran away, and was gone for four months before she was found. Part of her reasoning when she left was that we weren't going to find her. We weren't going to win this one, and she was going to do whatever she could to not come back. It was during this four-month period that Cristina became more heavily involved with drugs and alcohol, and made the bad choice of joining a violent street gang. To this day, there is still light scarring of the mark branded into her flesh by the notorious CRIPs.

Gang life can be brutal, and even though she ran with the

CRIPs for only a short period, she witnessed some horrific violence. One specific incident stands out in Cristina's memory. Sitting in a car, in a less-than-sober state of mind, she witnessed somebody getting jumped by a large crowd of people. They were ruthless as they laid into this guy, beating the crap out of him even long after he had lost consciousness. Cristina describes it like this: "It was like a colony of ants piling into a piece of candy, swarming all over it. It was just crazy." Our whole family knows how sensitive Cristina is to violence, so the fact she was able to watch the entire incident is surprising. She must have been on some pretty hefty doses of whatever she was taking to just sit and watch something like that without calling the police or trying to save the person who was being attacked.

Cristina keeps saying, "I didn't care at the time," and I suppose this is part of the effect the drugs had on her personality. I do, however, think Cristina was suffering severe depression as a result of PTSD, because she really *does* care about violence, and it normally freaks her out completely. It was almost as if she was so depressed that even though she normally couldn't bear to watch such violence, she was unable to generate a response to show she cared. Her frame of mind seemed to have a self-destructive aspect to it at the time.

Cristina started out hooking up with people she knew, who introduced her to new people. Her lifestyle allowed her to meet more and more people, until one day she realized she was hanging with folk she would never have had contact with before running away. Along with meeting new people, she was also exposed to different drugs, and began experimenting with them. Before she knew it, Cristina was using more drugs and alcohol than she knew how to handle. Xanax, hard liquor, and marijuana became part of her daily diet. It was at this point Cristina realized many of her new friends were part of a gang.

When Bundy and I asked Cristina about what had happened the day she decided to join a gang, she told us, "It was a spur of the moment thing... because my friend did it, I did it. Basically, we just met these people one day and we decided to do it." It was a simple exercise for girls to join the gang, unlike the violent initiation rituals men sometimes have to go through. If you are the girlfriend of somebody who is already a gang member, you can simply join. It doesn't even have to be a mutually exclusive relationship. As long as you're in with the crowd, you can just join the gang. What surprises me most is that Cristina was actually branded, and she still bears the scar from that experience.

Source: © 2018 Francis and Cristi Bundukamara
Order from left to right: Tallant, Nidra, Tallant Jr (TJ), Bundy, Reggie, Cristi, Kayla, Cory, Savanna, Miah, Cristina

Chapter Eleven: Human Trafficking is Real

As with the first time, the second time Cristina ran away was to be with a guy she knew from school, called Joshua. This time, however, after spending a short time together, they broke up. Eighteen years old now, she spent some time with one of her biological siblings, and hoping to get herself together, she enrolled in Job Corps. While enrolled there, a friend told Cristina about a job opportunity waiting tables in a restaurant, so they got all their friends together and had a meeting. When they followed up on this "job opportunity" it turned out there were no waitressing jobs. The man who was trying to recruit girls from Job Corps was actually a pimp, whose real agenda was to hustle these girls into being prostituted so he could make money from them.

These characters have a certain type of personality. They have a lot of charisma, which they use to flatter the girls into liking them, and then use this to control the girls. At this point, one of Cristina's friends, who needed her bills paid, actually did have sex with some random guy just to settle her bills. When

Cristina realized what was going on, she declined the offer, and the group of friends all separated for a while... but this guy was persistent. He was a good looking thirty-nine year old man, and Cristina was attracted to him, so when she refused his offer he came on to her, and got her to sleep with him. He then started pressuring Cristina to have sex with other men, making her believe she would be pleasing him by doing this. Knowing Cristina was attracted to him, he kept applying pressure on her to do things with random strangers that she never would have under normal circumstances. This is how these men operate.

Of course, he was taking all the money she earned as well. Not surprisingly, once Cristina was safe with us at home again, she found out this guy was wanted by the police for sex trafficking. This seems to be the way human traffickers work— they identify girls who are vulnerable and who are facing difficulty, and they target them. What many Americans don't realize is that you don't need to steal girls to involve them in the trafficking industry. Many TV programs seem to give the idea that sex trafficking is about stealing women, but this is not the case.

Most women and girls who are caught up in the trafficking industry are simply trying to please a charming and charismatic pimp they have fallen for. Once they are caught up in this world, it's very difficult to walk away. Cristina has a big heart and is very trusting, but I know Cristina is also gullible, and this is probably what caused her to believe this guy really cared for her. She wants to believe that people she cares about are telling the truth, but this sometimes leads her to care for people who don't truly care about *her*.

While driving with this guy who was pretending to be her boyfriend but who was really just her pimp, they were involved in an accident. They fled the scene, hoping to convince the authorities that somebody had stolen the car, but the guy whose car they had hit had taken a picture of them. Once the cops had tracked them down they searched Cristina's bag and found a stash of drugs, including marijuana, Xanax, and cocaine. Although Cristina was carrying all the drugs she was just a casual user, *not* a drug dealer.

In typical drug-dealer fashion, the man convinced Cristina to take the rap: "You just plead guilty to the charge," he told her. "You're young, you'll be out by tomorrow. Don't worry, I'll bail you out." So Cristina pleaded guilty to the charge. This guy was obviously an old hand at manipulating the system, and he was right in the sense that because it was her first charge, she *did* get out the next day. Interestingly, the bail bondsman was a friend of his, so the bondsman just posted Cristina's bail on the promise of a payment. Being eighteen, a consequence of Cristina pleading guilty was being released on probation. Then, a few months later, to my absolute horror I heard Cristina was being prostituted by this man. The worst part was, because she was an adult there was nothing we could do, even as her parents. Kayla actually told me what was going on. Cristina and Kayla's biological siblings knew what Cristina had been drawn into, and one of them told Kayla, who told me. She showed me a website with pictures of Cristina advertising herself, and as a mother, your heart just breaks... I mean, when you see that you feel so helpless, as if your hands are tied. You feel like you can't even save your own kid.

Even though I felt helpless, I was also desperate, so I called the police and asked them if there was anything I could do. I showed them the advertisement page and explained to them it was my daughter's life and reputation at stake. I honestly feel God led me to the website, enabling me to tell the police, which ultimately led to Cristina being caught. Victims who are being prostituted aren't high on the police department's list of priorities, but because I reported what I had found out, they did respond to the advertisement and went to her apartment.

When they found a whole lot of drugs on the premises, because she was still on probation for drug charges, she was arrested. Four felony charges were now added to the two original charges, and she was charged with prostitution, which is a misdemeanor. The thing is, prostitution is almost always associated with drugs. I mean, if you think about what it takes for a girl to be able to do that, most of the time she needs to be intoxicated. This being her second offense, Cristina ended up going to jail for a year. This experience gave Cristina a better understanding of the pimp who was abusing her. After three or four months in jail she realized this guy who she thought was her boyfriend was just using her, and that he really didn't care about her. It was a hard lesson to learn, as she now has a criminal record. With these new charges, Cristina ended up with six felony drug charges against her name.

Concerned this would follow her for the rest of her life, I advised Cristina to arrange some sort of plea deal because *she* wasn't the drug felon. But she wanted so badly to get out of jail she just pleaded guilty, and spent a year in jail before being released on two years' probation. Honestly, we yet again felt relief when Cristina was in jail; at least she was safe and off the streets. But then, to make matters more difficult, she was stuck in the Keys for another two years, completing her probation period. We're proud of Cristina for sticking to the rules and seeing out her probation without any added drama. More importantly though, she had an experience in jail that seems to have created a turning point in her life.

In Cristina's own words, "Jail is a very lonely place!" As

very often happens in life, we sometimes need to reach rock-bottom before we begin the journey back to a normal life. Having experienced the loneliness that comes with being imprisoned, Cristina started reading the Bible and spending time in prayer. As a result of opening herself to God's word, and opening a channel of communication to Him through prayer, Cristina has since told us that, "God kind of came to me in jail." I don't know if it was an actual visitation by God or if she just felt His presence as He started guiding her onto a healthier life-path, but these details don't really matter. What matters is that Cristina developed a personal relationship with God, and as a result of her experience her life was slowly but surely put back on track. This has really put my heart at ease, and Bundy's, because while we were all living through this ordeal it was heart-wrenchingly painful for us as parents.

Cristina also told us her desperate, careless approach to life had actually started after Johnny's death. His death left her feeling empty, with no hope for the future. Cristina really does try to stay positive but she also swings from being positive to feeling hopeless. She was still struggling with Johnny's death, and then Kayla started rebelling and went to Teen Challenge, which was another trauma for her—almost as if now she had lost another sibling.

We realize now it was probably a mistake sending the girls to Teen Challenge, but we honestly didn't have many options to keep the girls from running around on the street. In the final analysis though, Teen Challenge was not helpful. With Kayla's Reactive Attachment Disorder, she has a really hard time attaching to people, and there I was, saying, "I love you and I want you to be a part of our family but I'm going to send you to this program for nine-months-to-a-year." That's an eternity to a child. It was a Christian program, but I just don't think it was the right choice... however, I still don't know that there was any other choice. We couldn't just leave them to keep running away. I fully understand why Kayla called it the "Jesus jail."

Cristina's time in jail gave her an opportunity to start reading her Bible and praying more. In turn, this led to a better understanding of how she was being manipulated, and gave her the strength to walk away from that lifestyle. And yet, her time in jail brought other difficulties. As she recently admitted to Bundy and I, having no control over her surroundings was difficult to deal with. When she first went in, right in the beginning of her term, one of the other girls tried to touch her inappropriately, which really freaked her out. She was desperate to get away from this nightmare scenario, and fortunately, one of her friends—a big girl who had been there for a while already—told the other girl to leave Cristina alone. "When you're in the system... when you're in jail," Cristina explained to us, "they don't really care about you. You have no control over anything. Your rights are gone." Thankfully, Cristina had a friend who cared enough to protect her.

When we first decided to write this book, Cristina didn't want her story to be included. She was understandably concerned about people judging her, even though they don't know her. Once she had given it more thought she changed her mind, telling us it was important to her that people read her testimony, so they would have a better understanding of what God had done in her life. This is what she told us: "I want to tell my testimony because I feel that people should know how God changed my life, and that without God and my family, I might not be here today. I was being selfish when I first said no. I was just concerned about how the message would be written." When I became aware of her concern, we talked more about how her story would be portrayed. I assured her she is not a monster, and people would admire her courage. "I didn't fully think about the lives that would change through hearing my story," Cristina told me, "and now I want people to know that no matter what you go through, anything is possible with God."

This makes me very proud of my daughter, and her change of heart actually made me cry, as it shows great maturity. I think Cristina finally understands that she fell victim to a human trafficker, and it is important for her to tell her story so other parents and children recognize that human trafficking happens in just about every city and town across the globe. It's a problem that affects both developed and developing countries... it's happening right here in America.

Source: © 2018 Francis and Cristi Bundukamara
Order from left to right: Nidra, Kayla, Cristi, Cristina

Chapter Twelve: Hope

Hope: what a difficult word in the midst of hardship. This word evokes so many emotions in me. Sometimes the word 'hope' brings joy, peace, and positive thoughts for the future; sometimes the word brings me to tears, as I ask for God's mercy on my family. "Now faith is confidence in what we hope for and assurance about what we do not see" (Hebrews 11:1.)

I refuse hopelessness. I choose to believe God is good. I choose to believe in both conventional and alternative medicine. I choose to believe in the good of people. I choose to ask for help and to surround myself with encouraging people. I choose to continue praying for the salvation of all my children. I choose to pray for deep emotional healing for Cristina and Kayla. I choose to continue praying for healing from DRPLA. I choose to continue to research, seek out, and try various treatments for Reggie. In our family, Reggie is the most afflicted by DRPLA, and when we find successful treatment it will also help Miah and Bundy. Through perseverance, prayer, and research, I find a way to never give up. Hebrews 10:23 gives us excellent advice: "Let us hold unswervingly to the hope we profess, for he who promised is faithful." We choose to live out our hope in very active ways. The following are examples of how the Bundukamara's choose to experience and live in hope.

During my research of traditional, experimental, and alternative treatments for neurodegenerative conditions, I came across many proposed treatments for DRPLA or its symptoms. We were willing to try any reasonable treatment to give our son a better life. One of these was the ketogenic diet, a stringent and precise high fat and protein, low carbohydrate diet. Results have shown how this diet can reduce and even stop seizures in some children. Research also showed the ketogenic diet can slow down the progression of degenerative disorders, so we put Reggie on the diet twice, each time for a year and a half. We really believed the diet would make a difference in Reggie so we stuck to it, even though the preparation of each meal is onerous, and it's not a fun diet for a kid.

In our efforts to try everything we believed was

promising, we raised $20,000 to take Reggie to Mexico in 2010 for a stem cell transplant. We felt very strongly a stem cell transplant would reverse the symptoms Reggie was experiencing. Many people around us believed in the treatment too and were very generous in their support. Bundy's best friend gave $1,000, my parents $1,000 each, and other friends gave several hundred each. We started a blog and video update to provide feedback to the donors, and to record Reggie's condition before and after the treatment.

Reggie seemed to improve for three months after the stem cell transplant, and then became significantly worse. By January of 2011 Reggie had declined to the point where he was doing very little walking and was having trouble eating. There is a lot of hope in stem cell transplant medicine, but looking back I can see why it didn't work when targeting a genetic condition. Reggie's own stem cells were used and yet, for the treatment to be effective, I believe there would need to be a healthy donor and a specific vector involved that would help to cross the blood-brain barrier. There is, however, still a lot of hope in the future of stem cell therapy.

In May later that year, we took Reggie off the ketogenic diet. It wasn't helping his seizures and he was having difficulty eating. With all Reggie was going through, I felt bad that not even his meals were tasty. Planning forward I decided to not initiate the ketogenic diet with Miah and Bundy, and let them eat whatever they wanted. The following month we recorded Reggie having five grand mal seizures in one day, but this became a normal occurrence so we stopped recording the frequency of his seizures. Reggie's seizures were sometimes progressive; starting with little ones they progressed into a big seizure, but then on some occasions it was just—bam!—a big one. Discouraging, but we didn't give up hope.

Previously we had tried Reggie on a course of hyperbaric oxygen therapy (HBOT), a therapy which involves breathing pure oxygen in a pressurized tube. It seemed to help him so we began another course of HBOT, but at around $200 a session it is difficult to maintain financially. Reggie's condition declined further to the point where he was hospitalized for two weeks to address his pain, seizures, and weight loss. We eventually consented to having a feeding tube inserted because he kept losing weight and we couldn't control the seizures enough for him to eat.

Reggie's seizure pattern was still two good days, one bad day, and in an effort to break this cycle we had a small pacemaker-like generator implanted in his chest wall, called a Vagal Nerve Stimulator (VNS.) The device is programmed to send regular, mild pulses of electrical energy to the brain in an attempt to control the seizures. We really hoped the VNS would work for Reggie, but unfortunately nothing we tried could break the cycle of two good days and one bad. Committed to never give up, we still had hope.

One of the days the pattern of seizures worked for Reggie was Christmas that year. Since the Christmas Eve breakfast of Reggie's first seizure we had not had a seizure-free Christmas. This truly saddened me, as Christmas was Reggie's favorite time.

He enjoyed the excitement of Christmas, and loved opening presents. Reggie's face shone with anticipation and pleasure as he tore the wrapping off his gifts. Laughing, we even suggested re-wrapping the gifts so we could all enjoy him opening them again the next day. That Christmas was like the old days when Reggie's laughter filled our home with happiness.

Many adult children have challenges when caring for their parents, but in true Bundukamara style, Pop Pops made sure our relationship wasn't typical. On one occasion he became angry and confused. We sent him for a psychiatric evaluation but they couldn't find any underlying reason for his anger and confusion. A few days later he returned to being his usual self—a funny and educated old man. Once he sat on the front porch, reportedly waiting to be picked up for a trip to Africa. As we tried to present reality to him, his anger began to escalate. That day he ripped up 2,000 dollars in twenty-dollar bills, which he pulled out of his packed traveling bag. Once again, he spent a couple of days in a psychiatric hospital. After this incident we realized we had to start treating him differently. We stopped arguing with him, and allowed him to believe he was going back to Africa. Every once in a while he would become infused with energy that was almost manic in its intensity, and he would stay up for days, packing for Africa. We would beg him to stay, telling him that Reggie needed his research brain to help find a cure for his illness. At this point it was all just to get him to calm down, as he was no longer functioning professionally.

As difficult as it was at times, we found a way to make caring for Pop Pops work. We chose to care. We chose to submit to respecting him as our family elder, even when he obviously didn't respect us. We chose patience. Bundy personally chose to forgive him for the many hurts he inflicted on him during his childhood. As a family, we chose to continually forgive his verbal abuse. We chose to see the good in him, like his love for Reggie and Miah. We chose to laugh at his comical side rather than focusing on the difficult side of his personality. We chose to believe he really did love us, which I'm sure he did, but just couldn't express it often.

Determined to live in hope, people often ask me how I do it, with some even insinuating I'm a "superwoman." Although the compliment feels nice, I am who I am by God's grace alone. I was a rebellious, self-seeking young woman with little self-esteem. God has used that rebellious spirit to give me the strength to never give up hope. Despite their DRPLA diagnoses, Reggie, Miah, and Bundy will be okay. Despite Cristina's felony charges and the things she has witnessed, she will be okay. God will use Kayla's rebellious spirit, as He has used mine. We will be proud of Cory, and God will use Nidra's strength in incredible ways. Even Pop Pops brought much joy and happiness into our lives. Bundy and I have accepted hope as a vital part of God's plan for living a full and productive life: "And now these three remain: faith, hope and love..." (1 Corinthians 13:13.)

Source: © 2018 Francis and Cristi Bundukamara
Reggie

Chapter Thirteen: Reggie Therapy

"We're experiencing God at work, Cristi!" Ruth was bubbling over with excitement as her face appeared in our doorway. "As I entered the classroom today," she continued eagerly, "not even properly through the doorway, I was bombarded with questions."

"How's Reggie today?"

"Did Reggie have a better day after we left?"

"Did he this… did he that?"

"And some of them have never met Reggie!" she exclaimed, her eyes shining. "So many people know about him it's mind-blowing." She suddenly remembered to give me a quick hug in greeting before she continued again.

"You know something important is happening when, after these Service Learning Fairs, you walk into a modern-day classroom of about thirty-five or forty students, and maybe just one or two of them actually came to therapy the evening before, but they're *all* talking about Reggie... that's God. That really is God at work, and we're experiencing it firsthand."

Shortly after Christina joined the CRIPs and was then returned to us, we sent her back to Teen Challenge to complete the program. Meanwhile, Reggie's health had started to decline. He was doing very little walking and having difficulty eating. Then, after a serious hospitalization, the doctors recommended hospice for Reggie. I felt angry that medical professionals wanted to give up. Reggie is our son, and we know he is a fighter. We chose rather to keep searching—to find something that would turn Reggie's health around—and the doctors' pessimism gave us new energy to save him.

So we started what we called Reggie Therapy, which is based on a neurofascial approach to therapy which was developed and practiced at Integrative Manual Therapy (IMT) Wellness Center. A fascia is a band or sheet of connective tissue beneath the skin that attaches, stabilizes, encloses, and separates muscles and other internal organs. The process uses people to lay hands on vital organs and other body parts to help the body improve its processing functions. I say "based on" a neurofascial process because it turned out to be so much more than this. Over the years, thousands of people came to help. Our regulars we called Reggie addicts, and we started a blog and a website to keep Reggie's followers informed.

Reggie Therapy ran for three years, and for the first year we did it every single day, non-stop, through the holidays—every day for a year—then we decreased it to three times a week. The sessions were an hour long, and the therapy was done mostly with college student volunteers. It was generally set up in the evening from 7 p.m. to 8 p.m., to accommodate people getting home from work. I taught a class called community service nursing, and the students were required to do service in the community. So they earned community service hours for coming out and trying Reggie Therapy, and then from there, people just kept coming.

Initially, I had students getting involved for service learning hours, but many people continued volunteering after their hours were complete. Ruth, who was not a nursing student at the college, told other students about Reggie and the entire process of Reggie Therapy, and this drew more students. We would also attend fairs called Service Learning Fairs, where we would recruit other students needing community service hours.

We had a room off to the side of our home where we gathered for the therapy, or occasionally we'd put Reggie's table in front of the TV set if there was a good football game on. I positioned certain people in specific places according to what best suited the requirements—the larger or stronger hands were placed underneath Reggie, while the others were focused on the top of Reggie's body. I chose very specific pinpoints to focus attention on—at times, it was his liver, or his brain, other times it was the heart or his lungs—because the therapy was very specific.

Reggie, sometimes had good days, when he resisted having to lie still for one hour, and some days would be bad days—when he had seizures, or he threw up or had diarrhea; but good or bad days, there were always willing volunteers. We sat around Reggie with our hands joined to different parts, like a giant Twister™ game, and did not move. We would scratch each other's noses and heads, and our standing joke—or only rule—was everyone had to wear deodorant, because we all got really close to each other.

The students called me Dr. B, and they would tell me what a unique experience Reggie Therapy was for them personally. Over time, as we got to know each other, and they got to know the process and Reggie, they began to feel it. You could literally feel the electrical impulses through your hands. Once, when Ruth was over at our home collecting her boys who I had picked up for her, she put her hand on Reggie's forehead and could feel the electrical current running through her hand. When she lifted her hand Reggie began to tic, and when she put it back the tics stopped. She sat with her hands on Reggie's head for three hours, feeling the seizure activity running through her hands like an electrical current. And sometimes it was painful.

I would place Ruth so she could do his chest area for cardiac or lung therapy. It was a specific area where Ruth could feel the impulses literally running straight through her hands. She picked up on whatever Reggie was going through, and she would deliberately switch hands or do something different and still pick it up, but it was painful. She sat there quietly for an hour, in pain, experiencing this. As Christians, we talk about picking up one another's burdens, and that is what this was. She felt she was interceding for our son and whatever pain he was going through.

Sometimes we would sit and talk during Reggie Therapy, and sometimes we would pray. Now and then we had pastors join us, and occasionally we would have prayer groups visit. It was profound and unique, and so, as semesters ended we noticed who the Reggie addicts were—the people who continued to come back—and often we would have very deep moments together. It was almost like group therapy for all of us—how we felt, how our day went, things like that. Especially when it was just women, we would open up. We joked about talking so much in front of Reggie that if he ever started speaking again we would be in trouble—because Reggie knew all of our secrets.

During one therapy session when we had about twelve people over, Pop Pops emerged from his room and shuffled past us in his underwear. We all watched as he went to the refrigerator, took something out to drink, and shuffled back to his room without saying a word. In fact, we laughed about whether he had noticed we were there at all.

Reggie Therapy had a profound impact on the people involved. The way we did it had probably never been done before, and it never would be done for anyone in quite the same way ever again. We've often talked about how these sessions became group therapy sessions for all of us and tried to pinpoint exactly why Reggie had such a powerful effect on people. When we first began Reggie Therapy, Reggie could barely talk, but even though he could only say a few words, he somehow developed relationships with people. Another topic we discussed was the wide-ranging scope of drama going on in the Bundukamara household—all happening at the same time—and how I, being the mom, had to manage these dramas, and what this looked like to my friends on the outside who were looking in.

When Reggie was hospitalized for fluid on his lungs in November of 2012 the doctor attending him recommended a permanent breathing tube. I absolutely refused. I had to argue with the doctor to give Reggie a surgery to prevent the aspiration of fluid in the lungs. I felt his recommendation was given in arrogance. He didn't know the whole story, didn't really look at all the tests, and just decided, "This is simply the next step in your disease process." A tracheotomy introduces infection, and putting someone like Reggie on a trach is making the situation worse. We felt a tracheotomy is something that could be an extension of life but would reduce his quality of life. I insisted on a second opinion, and thankfully the second doctor agreed with me. I often felt like I was fighting with doctors to get the treatment I knew would be best for Reggie.

In January of the following year, we had Botox put into Reggie's salivary glands in an attempt to reduce the aspiration on his saliva. This seemed to have a paradoxical effect and worsened his saliva, cough, and aspiration. At this point, Reggie was mainly feeding tube fed so we had four of his six salivary glands removed, which significantly improved his quality of life. Even though he wasn't eating anymore we would sometimes slip a bite of chocolate cake into his mouth for him to taste. His response was a big chocolate smeared smile.

As Reggie continued to decline I intensified my fight to help him. I stood firm on my belief that I would find something to make him better, but the cost of Reggie's care and treatments was becoming a severe strain on our family finances. Regular insurance does not cover in-home services, and if you don't qualify for Medicaid you receive no assistance at all. In desperation, we contacted a congressman through a friend of ours to get special consideration and eventually received help from the State of Florida with nursing care for Reggie.

Later that year, Reggie was experiencing extreme discomfort that made him scream for five days. Neither of us got any sleep during that time until he was admitted to hospital. The first diagnosis was thalamic storming, but later they called it dystonic attacks. Reggie's creatine phosphokinase (CPK) and liver enzymes were dangerously elevated so the hospital once more recommended hospice. Again, we refused. I remember distinctly the doctor coming in and saying, "Take Reggie home, love on him, there is nothing else we can do!" I must admit, some of my—what looks like hope and strength to everybody—is really arrogance, but the important thing to note here, and this gives me an edge over everybody else, is when you're non-medical you actually believe medical science is black and white, so most people agree with what doctors recommend. The reality, however, is that there *are* some facts these recommendations are based on, but there is also a lot of subjectivity involved. Much of our medical knowledge evolves and changes, and what we thought ten years ago is not what we know to be true today. So when, during that hospitalization, it was presented as an end of life event, any other parent—and I know this for a fact because I've seen people do this—would have submitted to morphine and death, because that is the only thing you can do to treat it, right? You suppress it enough for the person to stop breathing.

I watched a DRPLA boy go through that on the internet,

and I've seen a couple of moms I know go through it, and again, I said, "No, this isn't end of life, and no, you're not going to kill my son with morphine. We're going to figure it out; we're going to walk out of here." And each time we *did* walk out. More than once they said he was going to die on a specific day, and a few days later he was better. They told us to make our plans and arrangements, and then Reggie would walk out of the hospital on the day after they said he would die. This happened over and over again.

Everyone we were acquainted with knew we were constantly searching for new or different treatments we could try, in the hope of finding a cure, or even just to improve the quality of Reggie's life. Some of our more liberal friends suggested we watch a special on CNN™ about using cannabis in the treatment of epilepsy. I'm a conservative Christian, and would never have considered using cannabis, personally or on my son, so these suggestions were politely ignored. Then a few other people suggested I watch the show, but only after four or five of my friends insisted I watch it, some of them Christians, did I actually sit down and watch the show.

The CNN™ special documented the remarkable effects of CBD oil on children with epilepsy. I remember thinking, *Wow! This could be it!* It was exciting, but the show also highlighted the fact that the cannabis-based CBD oil they were using was only legal in Colorado. We couldn't order it to be delivered to our home in Florida, and if we went to Colorado to get some we couldn't bring it back or we might end up facing federal trafficking charges. This meant that if we wanted our children to benefit from the oil we would have to move to Colorado. The oil could make a huge difference in Reggie and Miah's lives, but moving home to a different state is an enormous decision, and not one taken lightly.

We considered what we felt were the most important aspects of moving to Colorado. I have a high critical need job, so I knew I wouldn't have difficulty finding work, and being a cool football-coach type of teacher, we had no reason to believe Bundy wouldn't also find a job easily. Reggie wasn't going to school as he was in a homebound program, so we could just get a tutor to come out to him. Miah was very sociable, so we had no concerns about the transition for her. The worst part of moving would be leaving our family, friends, and Reggie addicts. Our friends are such a big part of our lives, and they occupied a very big space in our hearts. Leaving them would be the hardest part of moving to Colorado.

Source: © 2018 Francis and Cristi Bundukamara
Cristi, Reggie and Reggie Addicts

Chapter Fourteen: Reggie Addicts

"It's Ruth," I called out over my shoulder to Reggie, who was watching football highlights in anticipation of today's game. I opened the front door and Ruth walked in.

"Hey, Cristi. Hi Reggie. Getting ready for the game I see." She kissed Reggie on his forehead and slung her bag over a chair. Reggie smiled lovingly at her before turning his eyes back to the TV screen. The intense love Reggie is able to project with his smiling eyes never ceases to amaze me. So many people have commented on this, so I know it's not just me being a devoted mom.

"Who else are we expecting for today's session?" Ruth asked, taking a seat opposite mine at the massage table.

"Narin and Henly should be here any minute," I told her. "Daniella, Crystal, and Frances will also be joining us, so seven in total."

"The usual suspects," joked Ruth. "Or should I say, 'the usual addicts'?" she added with a grin.

It was a standing joke among those of us who regularly attended Reggie's therapy sessions. Certain individuals genuinely seemed addicted to spending time with Reggie. They made themselves available whenever possible, some of them traveling a fair distance to be part of the group laying hands on Reggie. The doorbell chimed again, and I was first greeted by Daniella's subtle fragrance as she leaned in to kiss my cheek. "Hi Dr. B," she said, squeezing my shoulder as she made a beeline for Reggie. Daniella is an absolute babe! A beautiful Colombian woman who dresses well regardless of the occasion. Her heels clicked past me as she made her way to Reggie. She cupped his face in her hands, kissing him three times on the forehead. "I missed you, little buddy," she cooed at him, and they smiled at each other as she held his gaze. I had left the front door open, and hearing a knock and a greeting, I turned to see Narin and Henly entering.

"Hi Dr. B. Hi Reggie, Ruth, Daniella," Henly called out, nodding at each of us in turn. His voice, a deep baritone, offset Narin's quiet, gentle greeting. It often struck me how diverse a group us Reggie addicts were. Narin and Henly seemed to typify this characteristic. Henly's personality displays a certain machismo, fairly common among men from the Dominican Republic. Outgoing and talkative, he leaves you in no doubt of his opinion on any subject. Narin, on the other hand, has a small frame, and although he doesn't talk much, is always actively participating in the group dynamic, and really cares for Reggie. Both men are extreme Reggie addicts. I was initially quite surprised by Henly's love for Reggie—it didn't seem to fit his personality, but when he kept showing up, we soon realized he was definitely part of the inner circle.

Crystal and Frances arrived within seconds of each other, completing today's therapy team.

"Maybe a bit closer, so Reggie doesn't strain his neck," directed Ruth, who was addressing Henly and Daniella. They were moving the massage table to a spot nearer the TV set, so we could all watch the football game with Reggie while we held our hands over specific parts of his body. Crystal and Frances greeted Reggie and the rest of us as they entered the living room and made themselves comfortable. They are yet another example of our group's diversity. Crystal is super sweet, and is the kind of person everybody likes. She tends to listen to the rest of us babble without really offering any strong opinions. Crystal is so sweet you just can't help liking her. Frances is also very likeable, yet strongly opinionated and rather eccentric. She is an artist—outspoken and confident.

We gathered around Reggie, taking our seats according to where each of us would be focusing on the different parts of Reggie's body. Once each of us had placed our hands on Reggie, we were silent, tuning in to the task at hand. The football game had started, and I heard the excitement in the commentator's voice as Ryan Tannehill of the Miami Dolphins™ connected with Dustin Keller for a 22-yard touchdown. The excitement in his voice eased the silent concentration around the table, and Daniella, frowning slightly, turned to me and asked, "How is Miah doing, Dr. B?"

I considered her question for a moment then released a long sigh before replying. "Miah is doing okay, Daniella. The pattern of her seizures is fairly consistent. Something triggers her between 3 a.m. and 6 a.m. every morning. I suppose the advantage of this is that her seizures generally happen here at home." I offered Daniella a smile but I knew my eyes conveyed hidden concern. She smiled back at me then frowned again.

"But Dr. B, when we first started Reggie Therapy three years ago, Miah was still living a seizure-free life, so what..." Henly, who was sitting next to Daniella, nudged her with his elbow.

"No, its okay, Henly. I don't mind talking about it." I looked at Daniella. "Miah had her first grand mal seizure around mid-January of 2011. It was absolutely devastating! I can't even begin to describe the emotions I felt that day. I remember thinking back to the awful day just before Christmas when Reggie had his first seizure... At that point I was still hopeful it wasn't a big deal. We had no idea about what we were dealing with. After Miah's first seizure it was different. We were struggling to be hopeful, because we knew exactly what we were dealing with." Daniella held my eyes for a moment, nodded slightly, and then lowered her eyes to where her hands were resting on Reggie's abdomen. The football commentary was the only sound in the room.

"So what did you do then, Dr. B?" Frances broke the silence in her forthright manner, which helped break the tension that had crept into the room.

"Well, we spent several days in the hospital, running an EEG, and various other tests on Miah. The only positive action we could take was to start Miah on seizure medication." Frances acknowledged my answer with a nod and we all sat quietly again, watching the Miami Dolphins™, who were in the process of thumping the Jacksonville Jaguars™ in this preseason game.

I'll never forget the first time Frances took part in one of our Reggie Therapy sessions. I called Ruth shortly after Frances arrived, as she had suggested to Frances that she join us. "You better get over here, Ruth, because this one scares me." I couldn't help smiling as I remembered Ruth's description of Frances from those early days, almost three years ago. She had called Frances a "sailor-cursing pothead, atheist, Buddhist." Ruth had invited Frances and her mom, Lee, who had attended math class with Ruth in school. I recalled one particular session, where Lee had started chanting the Hindu and Buddhist "Om" syllable over Reggie, and Ruth and I had looked at each other as if to say, "What have we gotten ourselves into?" And yet, Frances is a typical example of the many people who were radically touched by God through their interaction with Reggie. Over time, just through Ruth and I sharing God's word at these therapy sessions, Frances and her mom had become staunch Christians. There were actually four people who became Christians during Reggie's therapy sessions. It happened naturally, with people asking questions around the therapy table, and as they began to understand more about God and the Christian lifestyle, so were they drawn into becoming believers. It was a very dynamic time in our lives.

"So, Dr. B, if Miah is on seizure medication, how come she still has seizures every morning?" asked Henly.

"The medication helps to control the seizures," I explained. "It keeps them more or less at bay but it's pretty powerful medicine, so it has some bad side effects. As the dose increases, so do the side effects. We had to find a balance between controlling the seizures and keeping the side effects to a minimum."

"What kind of side effects?" asked Crystal.

"About a year after starting the seizure medication Miah started hearing voices talking to her," I told Crystal, whose eyes widened in surprise. "I was really scared she was experiencing a psychotic break, which sometimes happens to patients afflicted with DRPLA." Crystal shook her head in sympathy. After digesting this information for a moment she asked another question, this time in a soft, shy voice.

"What were the voices saying Dr. B?"

"Miah thought it was the devil talking to her," I replied. "She thought he was telling her she was bad." A pained expression twisted Crystal's face, and she shook her head in sympathy.

"It was terrible at the time, and it obviously affected the whole family. It happened on a few different occasions. The voices would come and go intermittently, and we finally figured out it was due to a side effect of the medication." Crystal looked lost in thought as she considered what I had told her.

The beauty of these Reggie Therapy sessions was twofold: they brought physical relief to Reggie but they also had a powerful effect on many of the regular Reggie addicts. Crystal is the first to admit that spending time with Reggie drew her closer to God. I know she was a born again believer when she first joined us, but towards the end of the three years she attended Reggie Therapy sessions, the outward expression of her faith had definitely increased. I suddenly snapped back to my surroundings as Ruth, Henly, and Daniella all cheered loudly. The Miami Dolphins™ seemed to be taking this game away from the Jacksonville Jaguars™.

"And what about your other daughters, Dr. B? How are Cristina and Kayla?" Narin asked, after the cheers had subsided. I guessed he hadn't asked after Nidra because she was no longer living at home with us.

"Cristina and Kayla are well, Narin. After graduating from high school they both promised they would stay home and focus on making better decisions, which they have done."

"I bet that's been a relief, Cristi," Ruth interjected with a smile.

"Yeah, it sure has," I agreed. "It sometimes felt as if we were reeling from crisis to crisis, so when Cristina and Kayla matured into the sensible young women they now are, it definitely released some of the pressure Bundy and I were feeling."

We all watched the game for a few moments but I could see Crystal was still thinking about Miah hearing voices. "So, does Miah still hear that terrible voice, Dr. B?"

"No, Crystal," I reassured her. "It only happened a few times and then Miah stopped hearing the voices." Crystal nodded silently but still looked worried. Seeing this, Ruth opened a new subject.

"Tell us more about Miah's Make a Wish™ cruise, Cristi. I

remember Reggie's cruise was to the Bahamas, but where did Miah go?" I smiled at Ruth. She knew these details by heart but she was hoping to distract Crystal.

"Miah's Make a Wish™ cruise was a seven-day Nickelodeon™ cruise to the Caribbean," I told this special group of people dedicating their time and energy to my son.

"Wow!" Crystal responded. Her eyes lit up with delight. "Seven days on a cruise ship... that must have been fun!"

"It was great fun! And this time around, we managed not to lose any children," I added, chuckling at the memory of how I had panicked after losing Reggie on his Make a Wish™ cruise. Everyone laughed, and Ruth and I shared a glance—her tactic had worked. We were all having fun again. "Miah really enjoyed watching Blueman Group™, who performed every evening. She especially liked seeing her name in the LED signs that run onstage before the start of the show. We requested Miah's name be included beforehand, and it was a real treat to see her face light up when she saw her name flashing across the stage."

"Tell them about the slime," Ruth said encouragingly. "That slime story always gets me," she added, wrinkling up her nose in distaste.

"Well, on this one specific day, they had what they call a slime-fest on board the Epic—that's the name of the liner we were cruising on. Best of all, Miah was chosen to participate as the main candidate. It was messy but Miah and the entire audience had great fun."

"I'm sorry but being covered in slime is *not* fun!" insisted Ruth. "Do you think that would be fun, Reggie?" Reggie turned his eyes to Ruth and nodded, a mischievous smile on his lips. "Ah, you would like that, wouldn't you just!" she teased him.

"Oh, yeah!" I called out, as something came to mind. "I just remembered, Blueman Group™ actually called Miah up to the stage and made a painting specifically for her. It really *was* a fun evening." I thought back to that moment in time, and I was grateful we had been given the opportunity to spend this special time with Miah. It seems at times that all our focus and attention had been on Reggie during those early years of their childhood. It isn't that we favored him; we were simply consumed with finding a cure for the difficulties he faced. Once we knew what we were fighting against we became even more determined to find a cure, as we would automatically be able to extend this knowledge into helping Miah and Bundy.

We were nearing the end of our therapy session, and time was also running out for the Jacksonville Jaguars™, who were trailing far behind the Miami Dolphins™. I was still thinking about Miah's Make A Wish™ cruise when Henly's voice interrupted my thoughts. "Dr. B, if Miah only recently started showing the symptoms of DRPLA, does it mean she has a milder form of the disorder?"

"Not really, Henly. The fact that Miah experienced an early onset of symptoms means it's similar to what Reggie is dealing with. Just last year, Miah started having anxiety attacks, and her seizures were becoming progressively worse. In fact, Miah recently had her worst grand mal seizure to date. It was so bad she started turning blue... we had a really difficult time stopping the seizure and getting her to breathe properly." There were murmurs of sympathy from all the women around the table. Henly nodded but I could see he had another question.

"Dr. B, surely Miah would also benefit from this neurofascial therapy if she is struggling with the same disorder?"

"That's a great question, Henly. Miah started having problems in school, and with all these symptoms increasing, we did actually try a few sessions of neurofascial therapy on her. For some reason though, she didn't respond well to the therapy... at least," I clarified, "she didn't respond as well as Reggie has." I was still thinking about how to explain to Henly why the process didn't really work for Miah when Ruth summed it up.

"I think what made it more difficult for Miah to respond to the treatment is that she was almost a teenage girl when we first tried it. I think it's different for a girl to relax when you have all these strange people putting their hands on you. It can be very claustrophobic. We also had to make sure there were only women

176

involved in Miah's sessions, due to the intimate nature of this therapy."

"Yeah, that makes sense," Henly acknowledged.

"What we also realized at that time was how very unique this experience is for all of us involved, including Reggie. I think the way Reggie responds to this therapy is what has made it so profound. He so obviously enjoys these sessions, and that's what allows all of us to relax and be ourselves." We all thought about what Ruth had said for a moment, and in that space of time, I could see her words had triggered something in Frances.

"Well, as you all know, I find it easy to relax and be myself!" stated Frances, which drew some smiles and a few chuckles. When Frances has an opinion, you *will* hear it! As we all knew.

"Yes. Those are great qualities," said Henly, looking serious.

"The thing is," Frances continued, "when I first met Reggie and Dr. B, being myself wasn't quite what it is now. I really thought I was a spiritual giant, chanting mantras and striving to comply with the four noble truths. Little did I realize in those early days that spending time with Reggie and his family would have such a profound effect on my spiritual journey. Like most of you, I started Reggie Therapy so I could build up volunteer hours I needed for a class. And then, when I was done with my volunteer hours, I just kept coming back. People would ask me why I kept coming back, thinking I was getting nothing out of it, but they didn't know Reggie." Frances leaned forward to kiss Reggie's forehead, and he rewarded her with a beautiful smile. "At some point, I realized just how much I was benefitting from these sessions. I never felt duty-bound, I just enjoyed Reggie's company, and I wanted to be here. I became a confirmed Reggie addict." Frances smiled, and there was a distant look in her eyes that told us she was locked into that moment when she first recognized the important place Reggie occupied in her life.

"It was then that I started actually hearing what Dr. B and Ruth were saying about the God of the Bible—their words began penetrating my soul. I found that I preferred the message of absolute attachment we have to God through His Son, Jesus."

Frances seemed to suddenly remember not everyone in the room shared the same spiritual beliefs, and not wanting to isolate anyone, she changed tack. "Anyway, I think you guys all witnessed the change that has taken place in my life, so all I can say is, without coming to know the one true God, I simply would not be the prophetic artist I have recently become."

"That's beautiful, Frances," said Narin, looking at Frances with great admiration. "What are you working on at the moment?" he asked, no doubt having heard the rumor she was working on a painting of Reggie.

"Ah! Now that's a surprise." He looked disappointed, so Frances waggled her eyebrows at him and we all laughed, especially Reggie. "But," she added, "you guys will be the first to see it when I'm finished painting."

"I certainly look forward to seeing your painting, Frances," I said, knowing this would encourage her. "And I'm truly grateful to God that He sent you here to help Reggie."

"I think Reggie has helped me even more," Frances replied. "As I said, I would not have entered into a relationship with God if I hadn't been drawn here to meet Reggie and his family."

"I think we can all agree on how special these therapy sessions have been for each of us," said Ruth, whose statement was affirmed by everyone around the table. "You guys know firsthand how powerful these sessions have been, and how we all occasionally feel what seems to be an electrical current running through our hands as they rest on Reggie's body." There were murmurs of agreement—this topic had been discussed among different groups of Reggie addicts. All people are susceptible to electromagnetic frequencies, and this is what neurofascial therapy taps into. "I have sometimes picked up on the pain Reggie is feeling, and just to be sure I wasn't imagining it, I would deliberately switch hands, and even then, I would still pick up on Reggie's pain." Ruth is particularly sensitive in this area, which is why I often place her in positions where Reggie most needs relief. "The point I'm trying to make," Ruth continued, "is that the Bible directs us, as Christians, to carry each other's burdens, as this is the way we will fulfill the law of Christ.[5] I honestly believe that by helping to carry Reggie's burden, by interceding for him and taking on some of his pain, we are going beyond the physical realm, and tapping into a spiritual dimension."

"Even if we aren't practicing Christians?" Henly asked, looking slightly skeptical.

"Yes, even then, Henly," Ruth answered, giving him a warm smile. "If you step in to pick up someone else's burden, you are still fulfilling the law of Christ, even though you may not be aware of it." Henly angled his head to one side, and after considering Ruth's reply, he nodded slowly.

"Yeah, I suppose that would be true," he conceded.

The clock had finally run out on the Jacksonville Jaguars™, who finished with only four turnovers, being soundly thrashed 27-3 by the Miami Dolphins™. We knew this signaled that our session had also drawn to a close, but nobody seemed

---

5   Paraphrase of Galatians 6:2

ready to stop the session. Narin had obviously been considering what Ruth had said, because after I had turned the volume on the TV set down, he spoke into the silence. "I think it's really cool that we can fulfill a spiritual law by easing Reggie's burden."

"I hadn't really thought about it from that angle," I said to him, "but it does make sense... there can be no doubt Reggie always feels better after you guys have shared his burden." Reggie nodded enthusiastically, and we all laughed again. I dearly loved this special group of Reggie addicts, and my heart was content as we began moving the massage table to where it normally stood. The men were discussing the football game, saying how pathetic the Jacksonville Jaguars™ had been, and the women stood around laughing and chatting about their families and careers. It never ceases to amaze me how at peace with our world we Reggie addicts are after Reggie Therapy.

Source: © Dipp Photography
Reggie, the star of Daniella's wedding

Chapter Fifteen: Moving for Marijuana

Before watching the CNN™ special titled "Weed" I wasn't interested in the controversy around medical marijuana. I didn't even realize the word marijuana was slang, derived from the racist "reefer madness" campaign.[6] When it seemed as if this may be what Reggie and Miah needed I had to rethink my stance on the use of a plant which was illegal in Florida, where we lived, but used freely as a medicine in other states. The proper name for this plant is cannabis, which has been shown to have medicinal properties and potential treatment options for multiple conditions.

It's like my whole world view changed in a matter of days. Being a strong Christian, professional, conservative family—never even considering using cannabis—then leaving everything to move across the country to give cannabis to our children. It all started with a message from a friend telling me I should watch the CNN™ special and consider cannabis for Reggie. I was actually offended by the message, and thought it ridiculous. It took three

---

6   https://www.leafly.com/news/cannabis-101/where-did-the-word-marijuana-come-from-anyway-01fb The Origin of the Word 'Marijuana'

additional people recommending I watch the special before I found it on YouTube™ and watched the one hour program. I absolutely couldn't believe what I was watching, and began researching everything I could on the subject. I went from completely ignorant to well-versed in cannabis as medicine within a couple of days. I found a phone number online and called it probably a hundred times before a woman named Heather answered. Little did I know, this woman would change my life, and become one of my closest friends. She provided all the information I needed to make the decision on whether we move to Colorado or wait, for what could be many years, for medical access to cannabis in Florida.

Notwithstanding the claims that the cannabis plant has up to seven hundred medicinal uses,[7] it was at that time illegal to use in Florida in any form. Many Christians, however, argue that the word of God tells us the laws of the country we live in should be obeyed. Can something be a sin in one state and not in another? It

---

7 700 MEDICINAL USES FOR CANNABIS SORTED BY DISEASE
http://www.encod.org/info/700-medicinal-uses-of-cannabis.html

186

didn't matter, we needed to see if cannabis could help and we weren't willing to risk the legal ramifications of bringing it to Florida. Bundy and I both had very good jobs, strong community ties, and lived right next door to my mother and father. Our support system was superior, and we would lose a lot of that by moving to Colorado. In a very intimate prayer with God, I said, "If Reggie is ultimately going to die, I don't want to move." I feel strongly He said, "Go."

After watching the CNN™ special in late August, I traveled to Colorado in October to get residency established, apply for a medical marijuana Colorado State card, find housing, and apply for jobs. Everything came together and we officially moved in November. The support of our family, friends, and Reggie addicts was amazing. Many people came out to say goodbye, help us pack and prepare our home for renting out. They spent hours painting our home, doing deep cleaning, and performing minor repairs for free. I felt it was a strong confirmation we were doing the right thing.

The treatment we were interested in trying for Reggie and Miah is a cannabis oil called Charlotte's Web™. It has a high cannabidiol (CBD) content, which has proven to be effective at controlling seizures, and given the extremely low content of THC—the main psychoactive compound found in cannabis—it has been deemed safe for children to use.

The reason Bundy and I finally made the decision to move to Colorado is, after a thorough investigation into the CBD oil we became convinced it would help reduce Reggie and Miah's seizures; improving their quality of life. We were not plagued by moral convictions surrounding the use of cannabis extracts, as we had no interest in the recreational use of the plant. We felt why we would be using it was central to the issue.

Charlotte's Web™ CBD oil was developed by a group of brothers from Colorado—the Stanley brothers. After the incredible success achieved in controlling the seizures of a five-year-old girl called Charlotte, the oil, then called Hippie's Disappointment because it contained such low levels of THC, was renamed Charlotte's Web™ in honor of its first pediatric patient.

A not-for-profit organization was started called *The Realm of Caring Foundation*™, CEO Heather Jackson, whose son, Zaki, was the second pediatric success stories using the Charlotte's Web™ oil. The mission of the foundation is research, education, and advocacy of cannabis oil and its incredible medicinal value.

During our research into Charlotte's Web™ CBD oil, I came into contact with *The Realm of Caring*™, and with Heather, the organization's CEO. Heather became a close friend and supported us during our challenging relocation to Colorado. I distinctly remember sending Heather a video of Reggie, and she later admitted she fell in love with him before ever meeting him.

We met many people who had left jobs and family members behind in states where cannabis remained outlawed, or couldn't be used to treat children. While some had moved their entire families, others were split, paying rent and raising children in two states. The Colorado refugees, as we called ourselves, consisted of people from all walks of life—various religious and political backgrounds, and against popular belief, most were not personal consumers of cannabis.

As I think of our support system and the positive effect Bundy had in the South Florida community, I remember the big party we arranged for his forty-fifth birthday. Forty-five was his football number, so I wanted to have a party on his forty-fifth birthday, celebrating his life and the positive influence he has had on other people. Ruth and I planned this party for a year, and every waking minute we were not busy we were together making arrangements. Bundy's friends in Maryland even went to their college and begged for his old jersey. We had all the coaches he worked with, men from the church, students he had taught and coached, even his best friends from third grade came to the party. Bundy can honestly say that on the day he felt greatly respected and loved.

During this time Cristina was in the Keys doing her probation, and while she was there we made the decision to move to Colorado. So in the midst of us packing up to go to Colorado, I couldn't help worrying about my daughter, because the Keys is known to be a party area, and it's hard to get your life together when everyone around you is partying. But Cristina was definitely in a better personal space. She had a full time job—at some point she even had two jobs—so she was able to pay for a little apartment. She drank a lot while doing her probation, but she was being tested for drugs, so we at least knew she was living drug-free. If she wasn't clean they would have sent her back to jail. Even so, as her mom, I still wasn't convinced she was doing well, as all I saw was the heavy partying. But I had to admit, she was stuck there, and there wasn't anything she could do about it. Cristina ended her probation and left the Keys to join us at the start of our second year in Colorado.

As if moving our family across the country wasn't difficult enough, before we left for Colorado we discovered Pop Pops was experiencing medical problems. He couldn't tolerate the thirty-six hour drive to Colorado, so we planned for him to fly to Colorado once we were settled. Three of our friends, Ruth,

Shannon, and Mindy, a petite blonde who Pop Pops took to and dubbed "White Tiger," took turns to come past our home daily and care for him until his flight, which was scheduled to take place shortly after we left for Colorado.

Ruth's husband is a member of an emergency medical services team so he went with Ruth to bathe and change Pop Pops, and to make him comfortable. One morning they went past our home to see Pop Pops and to ensure he had all he needed, but when they opened the house he wasn't there. To leave our home, Pop Pops would have to go up a step, through the house, down a step, out the front door, and down another step—in his wheelchair! Stunned, they called Mindy and Shannon to explain they had lost the non-ambulatory man.

After calling the police they frantically began searching our home and the property. Our home was on a five-acre piece of land enclosed with a fence, so unless Pop Pops stood up and dialed the number to unlock the gate, he was still on the property. Mindy rushed over to assist them, and as she drove onto the property she spotted him way out in the back. They went down there and found Pop Pops sitting in his wheelchair in nothing but his winter coat, clutching his backpack which contained twenty pairs of eyeglasses, all of his medication—some of which he didn't take any more—several pens, and a hospital identification card from 1970.

They called 911 and began hydrating him. At the Miami Baptist Hospital Pop Pops was belligerent, insisting he was a doctor in Africa and wanted to return there. When he realized one of the nurses was Nigerian he leaned towards him and proposed that if he would get him out of there and on a plane to Africa, he would sacrifice a goat in the name of the nurse's family. Managing to maintain his composure, the nurse replied, "Doctor Bundukamara, as much as I appreciate the sentiment I cannot do that."

From the emergency room, Pop Pops was rushed into emergency surgery where the decision was made to have him fitted with a pacemaker. He managed to tolerate the surgery and hospitalization, and was later transferred to a nursing home for rehab, before being cleared to make the flight to Colorado. While at the nursing home Pop Pops picked up an infection, but instead of sending him back to Miami Baptist Hospital, they sent him to Jackson South Hospital. After performing a procedure, Jackson South Hospital sent him back to the nursing home, where he stayed until he was ready to fly. When he was discharged from the nursing home my mom took him straight to the airport and sent him to Colorado.

Almost a year later in Colorado Pop Pops needed to be admitted back into the hospital. I informed 911 of his medical history and that he had a pacemaker. A couple of hours later the doctor came in to tell me Pop Pops didn't have a pacemaker. I argued that he did have a pacemaker and that it was put in at Miami Baptist Hospital. The doctor proceeded by showing me Pop Pops' chest X-ray, which had no sign of a pacemaker. I didn't know whether to be angry or just laugh, as Pop Pops has always throws us for a loop. As it turned out, he didn't have a pacemaker any longer. Miami Baptist Hospital had fitted the pacemaker, but

Jackson South Hospital had removed it when he went in for the infection. The pacemaker was put in to stabilize him for the flight to Colorado, but he made the trip without the pacemaker, and never had one fitted again.

Shortly after we moved to Colorado, Cory joined us and started working for the Stanley brothers, helping to produce Charlotte's Web™. In March Reggie was featured in *People Magazine*, and it was towards the end of April that he was hospitalized and spent time in the ICU. During that month Miah's seizures began to get worse, but she had begun the CBD oil treatment and we clung desperately to the hope that the treatment would be effective in controlling her seizures.

The following month we bought a new home in Colorado, but then the realtor of the house we were renting began causing major difficulties for us and eventually told us to leave the house, even though the new home we had bought was not ready for us to move Reggie into. Reggie was sick, and he was in and out of hospital during that difficult period, but Reggie's nurse at the time was kind enough to allow us to move into her living room until the improvements to our new home were safe enough for us to move Reggie in. It is kind of crazy to think back on some of these times—a family of an ill, severely disabled, wheelchair-bound son, residing in the living room of his nurse for almost a month.

Reggie was again hospitalized for pain but nothing was found on the CT scan and he was discharged. The pain got so bad we took him back to the hospital a week later where we discovered that on the preceding visit the doctor had missed a fractured femur, clearly evident on the previous scan. By the time we discovered this, the fracture had disintegrated into a complete break. This was a devastating discovery, as hip fractures can be extremely debilitating.

Reggie's hypersensitivity to anaesthesia makes any surgery hard on him, and after the hip surgery he experienced various complications during his rehabilitation. His back curved into the shape of a C as the muscles of his spine contracted. Even though Reggie was just a boy, his quality of life was forever changed.

Reggie had a PICC line inserted to intravenously administer antibiotics at home. We also drove to Denver bi-monthly for an entire year so Reggie could receive IVIG treatment, which we were later able to change to subcutaneous IG (SCIG) treatment at home.

After Reggie was admitted to ICU several times for pain, the movement-disorder specialist and neurologist concluded Reggie was having severe dystonia attacks and recommended Deep Brain Stimulator (DBS) surgery. Denver Children's Hospital told us Reggie's illness was too complex to perform the surgery there and would need to be done under intraoperative MRI, available only at Cook Children's Hospital in Dallas, Fort Worth Texas. With our hope returning, we packed and made the twelve-hour journey to Texas.

The results were not at all what we expected—Reggie's seizures were reduced from three to six seizures every three days, to only a couple per month—which was strange, as there is no medical reason the DBS should have any effect on the seizures. The DBS however, had no effect at all on the dystonia. We were crushed! Bundy and I didn't know where to turn. What was next? Fighting off overwhelming anxiety, only our love for Reggie and the drive to never give up kept us from falling into hopeless depression.

We held on tightly through the wild roller-coaster ride of joyous hope and devastating disappointment. We had to choose to believe Reggie would get better, and that his healing was in God's plan. At the same time, a major rainstorm severely damaged the roof of our home and caused the entire structure to slip two feet down the hill. This was not covered by home insurance and cost us thirty thousand dollars to stabilize our home. These kinds of things happen to home owners all the time, but you would think with our overwhelming constant fight for life and hope we might be spared enduring the ordinary trials as well. This is life, this is hope, and we will endure, love, and choose joy.

Bundy and I were married shortly after my parents were

divorced. My youngest brother, Wayne, was twelve years old at the time, and by the age of eighteen, he was an alcoholic. Wayne is really a good guy, and my parents tried to help him over the years, but the alcohol and unpredictable mood cycles had prevented any real success in his life.

When we moved to Colorado, we had him come and join us there, and arranged a job for him growing the plants for the CBD oil. He did well for a while, then started losing control of his drinking. He was eventually fired for drinking at work, and he returned to Florida without saying goodbye to us. Several months later, I received a call during the night to inform me he had been shot in the chest and was being airlifted to the closest trauma center. He survived the incident and did really well again for several months.

When he began slipping once more, we made him the offer of coming back to Colorado, where I had arranged a masonry job for him. He accepted our offer to return, got along really well with his boss, enjoyed the work, and we were pleased to see his life had begun to take a turn for the better.

For Reggie, the move to Colorado was indifferent; he didn't need to adjust to school here, as they have a homebound program, so he just had a tutor who came out to our home. Miah's transition to the new school was fine—in fact, for Miah the move was excellent. For Bundy and I, the move to Colorado was a lot more complex. We were forced to make significant adjustments in our work lives, and from a cultural perspective. I was born and raised in Miami, and the enormous cultural change was a shock. People in Colorado are more reserved and not very sociable—our neighbors here still don't know us—whereas in Miami people greet with a kiss, and touch each other when they speak. It took us three years to make friends, and the first year was very depressing for me.

Because of my high-critical-need work, I had a job when I arrived. For Bundy, it was different; we thought it would be easy because Bundy gets along so well with people—he could apply and have his choice of jobs. It was a pretty big blow for him when he just didn't get any positive response. Culturally, there's not a need for the cool football coach-type teacher out here, they're not looking for that. I was concerned about how he was presenting himself because there was increasing evidence of DRPLA with mild ataxia and dementia.

It would be against the law to fire you for displaying neurological symptoms, but when people interviewing you don't know what the symptoms are, they're not willing to risk finding out. He's super friendly and has all the qualifications, but he received no positive feedback from any of the several districts where he applied. When we shared this with his first neurologist, he said, "You really need to go on disability."

Bundy is still angry at that doctor to this day, but it was a major turning point for Bundy—he doesn't have what he had in Miami, and sometimes I feel guilty about that. At his high school and surrounding community, Bundy was known, respected, as an esteemed teacher and football coach.

Bundy had to find purpose again, and being able to be an

effective father was a big thing for him. In Florida he was working and coaching all the time, and because he wasn't able to spend much time at home, he felt he wasn't being the father he should have been. Being at home he was able to spend more time with the children, and it meant a lot to him. He spent all day with Reggie and his nurse, and could drive Miah to school as well as pick her up after school, so he felt he had been given an opportunity to be a better father than he had been.

It also taught Bundy humility. In Florida, everyone referred to our children as "Coach Bundy's kids," or to me as "Coach Bundy's wife." He was this pillar who couldn't face being weak but now realized he was weak, and the Lord has made us weak so we will lean on Him for strength. After this revelation, he was honestly happy to call himself "Cristi's husband," instead of the other way around.

Source: © People Magazine
Cristi and Reggie
https://people.com/archive/medical-marijuana-kids-fight-seizures-with-pot-vol-81-no-11/

Chapter Sixteen: Expressions of Love

While nurses, family, and friends were caring for Reggie and Miah back in Colorado, I waited in a post-surgical waiting room on the other side of the country to hear word on Bundy. The surgeon had told me it was a simple procedure and shouldn't take longer than one hour... it was now five hours later, and still no word. While I sat waiting, desperate to hear some news about my husband, I recalled how the transplant teams at the University of Maryland had initially denied Bundy's application to donate a kidney to his only brother. Bundy has a really generous heart.

About a year-and-a-half after we had moved to Colorado Bundy donated his kidney to his brother, Adam, even though he and his brother weren't very close at the time. The transplant team treating Adam initially denied Bundy's application to donate, due to his DRPLA diagnosis. Although ethical reasons were cited, I fought for Bundy to be able to give his kidney to his brother. We obtained letters from various doctors and agreed to sign additional legal documents, so when no other donors became available, the transplant team agreed to the operation.

I feel so strongly about my husband's generosity of spirit because this is what makes him so incredibly different than most people. The surgeon finally came to the waiting room and informed me that Bundy was so muscular it had taken five hours of aggressive surgery to remove his kidney. He told me Bundy was doing well, and that the kidney had been transplanted and was already hard at work inside Adam's body.

Bundy knew his brother could die if he didn't give him his kidney. He didn't hesitate, choosing to help him because he could. Maybe he knew, deep down inside, that even though he was doing everything possible to help Reggie, his son was becoming increasingly ill. He was, however, able to help his brother—so he did it for both of them. Bundy gave Adam his kidney to make a positive difference in a family member's life. The operation was successful but sadly, about a year later we discovered Adam had developed brain cancer. Adam was diagnosed with the same post-transplant cancer Adam and Bundy's mother had died from twenty-five years before. Organ transplant patients run the risk of B-cell proliferation after the transplant, and this is what happened in Adam's case. His B-cells evidently mutated, rendering them malignant, which resulted in a lymphoma. Of course, Adam knew the risks involved beforehand, but he didn't really have an option. Personally, I felt extremely proud of Bundy for sacrificing one of his kidneys to prolong his brother's life. It reveals my husband's absolute willingness to help people, even at his own expense—a true expression of love.

When Bundy found out Adam had developed brain cancer, he felt scared. He was afraid his brother was going to die, and felt a pressing need to go and see him. We decided to travel to Maryland to visit Adam, which was a great encouragement to him, and he told us how much our visit had motivated him. Ignoring the expense involved, we poured out our love on Adam, just as God expects of us, especially when it involves members of our family. Bundy was struck by how strong and brave, and wonderful his brother is. He was reminded of how he and his brother had been raised to be tough—especially after hearing Adam had gone from bed-ridden to walking in only four days after undergoing major surgery. His real name is the same as Pop

Pops'—Moses Abram Bundukamara—but he prefers Adam. Adam loves nicknames. He calls Bundy "Brooke"—his own personal expression of love. After enduring multiple hospitalizations, chemo, radiation, surgeries, and discontinuing his anti-rejection medication, Adam is doing well, and is planning a trip to visit us in Colorado.

People often ask how we manage to stay positive, even though we face so many challenges every day. They wonder how we can still go out of our way to help other people. The truth, I suppose, is that we specifically *choose* to help others. Life is about choices, and at some point we realized that choosing to sacrifice our time, energy, or money is actually just choosing to move forward selflessly. We are really just ordinary people, given extraordinary strength, hope, and love by God.

Shortly after we moved to Colorado Kayla also joined us, and immediately went online to find a boyfriend. She started dating an army guy named Jesus, and moved in with him. From the outset they fought a lot, and when Kayla got pregnant we all hoped their relationship would improve. Jesus withdrew from his position in the military, and they moved to Florida together. Sadly, however, their relationship continued becoming more toxic. The young couple was living with Jesus' family in Miami when Kayla gave birth to Alexandra, a lively baby girl. Even though there were clear signs her relationship with Jesus wasn't going to work out, Kayla really *wanted* it to work, so she chose to stay with him. When Kayla finally came to the realization their relationship was doomed she moved back to Colorado with Alexandra. The first thing she did was to go back online to look for another boyfriend. Then Kayla started bringing different men home.

One day we sat her down and told her she couldn't bring just any man home until she was serious about their relationship—he had to be someone who shared her hopes and dreams for the future. Kayla took our advice and found a suitable partner, and now has a long-term partner who I believe is good for her and Alexandra. Kayla really has matured a lot since becoming a single mother, and for the first time I feel she is going to be okay.

I suppose the craziest part of our family's story is that nothing ever happens in isolation! Just as Kayla seemed to finally be settling down, Cristina completed her probation in the Keys, and moved to Colorado. She completed a Certified Nurse Assistant (CAN) program, got a full time job, was attending church and sharing her testimony of God's provisions—especially while in jail. So we were somewhat surprised when she announced she was pregnant, and that there wasn't any indication Cristina and the father would have a meaningful relationship. Like any caring mother, I want more for my children. Bundy was simply angry, and it took a while for him to think of Cristina as a mother. He felt she was making up lies about the baby's father and was embarrassed about her defiant attitude regarding sex outside of marriage. Bundy and I recognize that how we respond to life's challenging circumstances ultimately defines who we are. Bearing this in mind, we chose to continue expressing our love and support for our daughter, and chose not to judge her. We choose to focus our expression of love on a genuine relationship with God, rather than the "rules" we believe God wants us to live by. It's not just Cristina—we have five grandchildren, and are currently planning our first wedding. Every day, we choose to display our relationship as an example of biblical marriage—we choose to show our family what it means to be a healthy example of husband and wife.

Nidra, meanwhile, had bought a home in Florida and was doing well. Her daughter, Savanna, was already ten years old at this stage, and her son, Tallant Junior (TJ), was eight. TJ registers on the autism spectrum and is currently using hemp CBD oil and doing really well. I believe the small rift in our relationship that developed when she first found out she was pregnant has been put behind us. Nidra taught me that conception is never a mistake, and I am grateful to her for showing such wisdom and maturity. She really is a great mom.In November of 2015, at the ripe old age of ninety-three, Pop Pops finally went to be with the Lord. We believe he began a relationship with God toward the end of his life. Pop Pops really loved singing, and he would sing with great opera-style gusto on Sundays alone in his room. I'm sure the neighbors could hear him. In spite of the many difficulties we faced as a result of our decision to take care of him, the love and laughter he brought into our home definitely outweighed these challenges. Our decision to take him into our home was a choice we made to share Jesus with him through our actions.

In Colorado we were able to apply for resources and get nursing assistance to help us care for Reggie. Although it was mainly Reggie who the nurses cared for, Miah sometimes needed their assistance as well. Before we received the results of the genetic tests done on Miah, I had strongly believed she had not inherited DRPLA. I clearly remember the day Miah had her first seizure, which happened even before we moved to Colorado. I was in shock, holding my little girl as the seizure shook her. I knew in the moment that this was not just a seizure—it was DRPLA winning the fight. Bundy had gone to work already so I was home alone. I called him and told him to take the day off and get home as quickly as he could, then called my office and told them I wasn't coming in. Miah slept while I waited for Bundy. As Bundy pulled up, I walked outside to tell him what had happened,

212

and we broke down crying. Clinging to each other in anguish, we fell to our knees on the grass in the front yard. Later, when Miah woke, we took her to the hospital, but there was nothing new they could tell us—we knew what this meant.

Miah's seizures continued to worsen, and a year after we moved to Colorado she had a really bad seizure; she lost her balance, and fell forward onto her face. When Miah came around she had broken her front teeth, had a busted lip, and a swollen eye. Shortly after this incident, Miah was hospitalized for the increased number of seizures she was experiencing. Her EEG reading recorded over three hundred seizures in a timespan of fifteen hours. It is so heart-wrenchingly difficult for the entire family to witness the steady decline of our loved ones. People sometimes ask me how I cope with the knowledge that my husband and two of my children are living with a terminal disease. How do I begin to answer? I have learned to try to live in the moment and to be grateful for God's mercies, which the Bible tells us are new every day.[8] We also choose to make good use of the time we have together. Miah's sweet sixteen party is a good example of this, as the party was great fun! We rented a club, hired a DJ, and lots of people celebrated with us. Everyone agreed the party was a huge success. Four months later, however, Miah was admitted for another EEG, and once again, the reading recorded hundreds of seizures. Not knowing what tomorrow will bring keeps us ready and primed for whatever life throws at us. It also allows us to live within the fullness of every moment.

Letting Go, the Ultimate Expression of Love

I must admit though, none of us were prepared for that fateful day a group of us gathered together for Reggie's final session of Reggie Therapy. As stated in the first chapter, Reggie was having a bad day. Reggie had experienced bad days like this before, so while I wasn't too worried, I definitely was concerned. As usual, after that day's Reggie addicts had been to administer his therapy, Reggie was feeling better. The day nurse left our home at six

---

8   Paraphrase of Lamentations 3:22-23

p.m., and when I returned to where Reggie lay, I noticed he was struggling to breathe, so I fitted the oxygen mask to his face. I had been wrestling all day with the idea of calling 911. After much deliberation I chose to follow the safest option and make the call, knowing rescue workers would take Reggie to the emergency room. Bundy had gone outside to make sure the rescue workers knew which house was ours, while I sat indoors with Reggie, who had started hyperventilating. Trying to test the level of oxygen in his blood, I became increasingly anxious as I struggled to coax a reading from the pulse oximeter I had fitted to Reggie's finger.

The rescue workers arrived, and while they were attaching their machine to Reggie, my friend, Heather, arrived. Although Heather is a great friend, showing up at my home at night isn't typical. God knew I needed her, and He put an urgent panic burning in her heart so she would visit my home that night. Heather arrived shortly after Pastor Bob. Realizing how serious Reggie's condition was, I left the room, hoping the rescue workers would find a way to save my son. I started praying, but honestly, I knew this was it. At some point I recall the rescue workers saying there was nothing more they could do. They asked if I would consent to them calling an end to their treatment of Reggie, as he was not responding. I refused, unwilling, and literally unable to give my consent. So they continued trying to resuscitate Reggie... but to no avail. Reggie was dead. He died suddenly, against my firm belief that not only would he live to see his eighteenth birthday, but that we would one day find a cure for Reggie, Miah, and Bundy. The only consolation to be had was that Reggie didn't suffer in those final moments. He died on his own terms, peacefully, quickly, and without having to experience the extreme pain he so often endured. There are no words to describe what I felt when seeing my son's lifeless body, while police and rescue workers prevented me from touching him before the coroner arrived, hours later. Physically, I was in shock. I felt an indescribable sadness, but I was not really feeling the full impact of it yet.

When the rescue workers arrived, Cristina, Kayla, and Wayne had come out of their rooms. Cristina had Nidra on the

216

line while Kayla was calling other family members. Cory told Kayla he would come right over, and he arrived before Reggie's body was removed. Nidra stayed on the line, and we were all present together in grief. Except Miah—Miah was asleep in her room, and we chose not to wake her. I mainly didn't want her to see Reggie's body, but I also didn't have the emotional strength to care for anyone else. I stayed up all night, talking with family members on the phone. In the morning, when Miah woke, Bundy and I told her together that Reggie had passed in the night.

Thank God Heather and Pastor Bob were there. Heather took emotional control of our home, coordinating police and rescue workers. She also ensured my greatest, pre-planned wish was accomplished—that of donating Reggie's brain to the Harvard Brain Bank for research. To our surprise, neither the rescue workers nor the coroner's office knew the process for donating organs. Heather immediately searched her phone, and even though it was after midnight, she called the *Harvard Brain Tissue Resource Center*. She not only got a hold of them, she completed the paperwork and coordinated a pathologist from

Denver to come to the Colorado Springs Coroner's Office to remove Reggie's brain. Just like his daddy, Reggie got to give an expression of love through organ donation. Pastor Bob was thankfully present for Bundy and Wayne, as I was just pacing, holding one of my favorite pictures of Reggie. My expression of love was letting go... I could not wish Reggie back to the daily pain he experienced, knowing he was now free.

A few days later we held a memorial service for Reggie, where we all came together in our grief. Everyone wore Spider-Man® attire and the room was filled with joy and color. I chose not to speak at the memorial service, so I could stay focused on God and be strong for my husband and children. Bundy spoke about John 13:7,[9] explaining that while we may not yet understand God's plan, we would at some stage. He also spoke about Reggie being a fighter, who had taught him many things. Reggie taught him to be like Job of the Bible, who never turned away from God. Bundy admitted that, in the beginning, he didn't

---

9   John 13:7 "Jesus replied, 'You do not realize now what I am doing, but later you will understand.'"

want to be like Job, but he now does want to be like Job, and keep praising God.

Miah spoke of how much she would miss Reggie, and Cory spoke about how many times we as a family had to watch Spider-Man®! He spoke about how Reggie never stopped moving, that he was the center of the family, and how—before he got sick—he would always be playing, non-stop, making us all laugh by giving a few comical examples. Kayla started with, "I met an angel when I was only nine years old," continuing with, "Reggie was the meaning of love," and then described his following of people around the world. Cristina read a poem, then pointed out that Reggie's memorial service fell on what would have been Johnny's 25th birthday, and that she pictured them hanging out together in Heaven. Nidra encouraged us with a quote from the original Spider-Man® movie: "Whatever life holds in store for me, I will never forget these words: with great power comes great responsibility. This is my gift, this is my curse, who am I?" This is Reggie and his power is to bring people together. We sang "Your Love O Lord," followed by "Our God is an awesome God." We then sang "Cry out to Jesus," and finished with "Big Big House," all of which were Reggie's favorites. Many people expressed feelings of joy after the memorial service. Heather described it as "grief and praise."

We also held a celebration of Reggie's life in Florida a few months later, where Frances the Reggie Addict created a prophetic portrait of Reggie for everyone to sign. We praised God for blessing us with Reggie, and we thanked Him for the seventeen years of love we had shared with this beautiful child He sent to us. Everyone loved Reggie, and his sudden death left a ragged, gaping hole in all of our hearts. I have lost two sons now, and while I also stand to lose Miah and Bundy, I continue living in hope. While I keep living in hope I still allow my adult children and grandchildren the freedom to praise God, to question Him, or even to denounce Him. People must always make up their own minds about what they believe. No matter how we respond to the hardships of life, or express our love, we are all proud to be members of this Bundukamara family.

Source: © National Geographic Magazine
Miah and Reggie
https://www.nationalgeographic.com/magazine/2015/06/m
arijuana-science-drug-research-legality/

Chapter Seventeen: With Great Power Comes Great Responsibility

Cristi's Final Letter to Reggie

"To my dear son Reggie,

Words cannot express how much I love you. A flood of feelings come over me when I try to describe your personality and what you have meant to me. As I look at pictures from your early childhood, I remember my ignorant feelings of blissfulness. I remember truly believing the scripture that says, "Train up a child in the way he should go, And when he is old he will not depart from it" (Proverbs 22.) I believed that if I followed God's law and was a good parent, God would protect you and you would grow up to be a healthy man of God. As I lifted you up in covenant Baptism, in the deepest recesses of my heart I gave you to the Lord, truly believing He had great things in store for you. Honestly, if I knew your years would be numbered to seventeen, I would not have been so willingly submissive to God.

As I look at your pictures from the age of five

through to twelve years old, I can't help but smile. You were a precocious boy with lots of energy and lots of love. We did so many fun things—horseback riding, swimming with the dolphins, riding roller coasters, endless hours in the pool, repetitive trips down the water slide, bike racing, vacations, cruises, even missionary work. I remember you counting to ten in Spanish while swimming with the street children in Mexico. You had a really good life, and I'm glad I spoiled you.

As I look at pictures from the last five years, I see the progression of DRPLA taking my boy— ever so slowly, but way too fast. There is a heavy, crushing weight on my chest... I desperately want to say I am so sorry, Reggie. I did my best, but my best wasn't good enough. I'm sorry for the precious, wasted time and energy we spent on aggressive treatments that didn't work. I didn't know and I had to try. I'm sorry that I am not smart enough to find a cure. I'm sorry it became increasingly more difficult for me to hold you. It hurt my heart so much when my touch no longer soothed you. I am sorry I struggled to maintain my hope. I am sorry I spent so much time and energy angry with God. I'm sorry I didn't take you to the emergency room that fateful day. I'm sorry I continued believing you would be healed, and never said goodbye.

As I grieve and wrestle with God over your death, I have to remind myself daily that you are happier now than any passing happiness I could ever have provided. If I truly believe what I say I believe, then I should be happy for you and look forward to eternity in Heaven with you, but my heart aches. If I believe what I say I believe, then I have nothing to be sorry about, and I should be able to rest in God's perfect plan. I ask God, "Why do I have to feel so much pain? Why is there such a disconnect with the heavenly realms? I lie down at night and ask God to allow me to dream of the heavens and to see your happiness, but I wake with just my faith. Reggie Josiah Bundukamara I love and miss you so much!

All my love,

Mom."

On that fateful evening, when Reggie's condition began rapidly deteriorating, Bundy thought the rescue workers would bring him back. He couldn't believe his boy, his Rubber-Man, didn't bounce back. Reggie always bounced back. When it hit Bundy that Reggie wouldn't bounce back this time, he could no longer function. A deep sadness overwhelmed him as he tried to go about doing his daily functions, knowing Reggie was no longer in our home. "I'm being selfish," Bundy admitted to me. "I don't want to give up my son." I completely understood the difficulty my husband faced in giving up his boy. I too was struggling to come to terms with our loss.

How *did* we come to terms with our loss?

As part of my grieving process, I committed to reading my final letter to Reggie to all the people interested in his story—to every person willing to listen. The more I read this letter, the more real my son's death has become, and each time I re-read it, the less emotional my reaction to it. I have also made a video to share with all the Reggie Addicts and his many followers.

People talk of "acceptance" and "closure" as part of the process when grieving the loss of a loved one, but in my case, I feel this is the wrong terminology. Although I do accept Reggie is no longer here on Earth with me, the goal I hope to attain through the grieving process goes beyond closure in the usual sense. I am looking for more than an emotional conclusion to a difficult life event. I don't simply want to relegate Reggie to memory—I want to keep alive the hope I will see him again when my spirit leaves the Earth. What I hope to achieve is a better understanding of life and death, and how they relate to eternity; and how I can start living for eternity while still walking the Earth.

People say losing a child is the most difficult thing anyone could ever go through; I've lost two children and may lose another. As I wrestle with this fact, only one thing comes to mind—there has to be something more... I have a simple message to share with anyone who struggles with what to believe: Is there a God; is there a Heaven; is there a Hell? Please *don't stop* seeking and searching. Eternity has been set in your heart;[10] please continue to search for the truth.

Meanwhile, I am trying to figure out how to move forward with my life while knowing Miah and Bundy are both still struggling with the debilitating effects of DRPLA. I fought very hard for Reggie and lost. I won't be able to fight the same way. While fighting for Reggie I really believed I could cure DRPLA. I now accept that without a miracle from God, it's unlikely I will cure DRPLA. Many people believe I should stop fighting—that God wants me to stop fighting—but this just makes me cry. I suppose my desire to be in control is really about *not* trusting God. After all, the worst has happened and it's not so bad... It sometimes seems clichéd, but I know I haven't lost him forever.

Today I have decided to fight believing I can win. I choose to fight differently now. I will fight for our happiness, trusting in His perfect plan. I will continue to investigate every

---

10   Paraphrase of Ecclesiastes 3:11

new medication and therapy, making every day matter, and living life for eternity. I may never cure DRPLA, but I will never give up hoping and I will be happy in the process. The Bundukamara's will continue to say I am Mentally STRONG™.

The night Reggie died I felt a range of emotion. His death shocked me to my core—it was utterly unexpected. Shock was followed by anger... How could this happen? Once I began to process the reality of my son's death, shock and anger gave way to a deep, unimaginable, and indescribable pain.

In coming to terms with my grief, I chose to wrestle with God in a very personal way. I believe God recognizes the intentions of our hearts, and He must have understood the sincerity of my plea when I asked Him why Reggie died despite my prayers for his healing. God has spoken to my heart twice so far in this regard.

The first time occurred while I was in prayer before God, sobbing, and begging for Reggie's forgiveness. I somehow believed Reggie knew all my sins and mistakes. In the midst of my tearful prayer, God gently said to me, "Reggie saw you like any young child looks to his mother—he saw you as perfectly loving to him. Reggie is not omnipresent nor omniscient, only I know the details of your heart."

The second time I was crying yet again during my prayer session. I was questioning God about those verses in the Bible that suggest you can ask God for anything and you will receive what you have asked for.[11] I had obviously asked, begged, and pleaded with God for years about healing Reggie, and I wanted to know why my request had not been answered. While I did not receive the answer I was looking for, I was given an even greater gift. In the gathering silence I heard God's gentle voice saying, "Ask of the heavenly realms." I started rationalizing in my prayer to God, and then it happened. God allowed Reggie to communicate with me. "Mom you think you are so smart, but you have *no idea*. I'm okay; Dad and Miah will be okay. And you're okay." These are not words I would have said to myself—the

---

11   Matthew 18:19; Matthew 21:22; Mark 11:24; John 14:13; John 15:7; John 15:16; John 16:23-24; James 1:5-6; James 1:17; 1 John 3:22; 1 John 5:14-15

words, the tone, the inflections were all clearly Reggie and expressed his personality. Reggie and I had communicated with body language and non-verbal cues for years, so I knew it was him who, with God's help, had conveyed this message to me. It was only a moment in time and there are no words to completely describe Reggie or the heavenly realm, but I can say with certainty that Reggie has a supernatural contentment. In that moment I experienced a peace that surpasses all understanding, and I try to reflect on that moment when I continue to experience the natural grief I still feel here on Earth.

I know some people might think I imagined this conversation, or even worse, that what I experienced was *not* a gift from God to put my heart at ease concerning Reggie's happiness and well-being. I wasn't communicating with Reggie, I was communicating with God, and he allowed Reggie to participate. Surely God is able to convey a son's message of comfort to his grieving mother from beyond the grave? Could it have been an "audible vision," where God allowed me to hear from Heaven—just that once—to ease my grieving? I have

231

actually heard stories of God giving people visions, or taking people to Heaven to see a family member who has passed. Some of my fellow believers would say those experiences are not from God, other believers might encourage such experiences. Perhaps Reggie asked God to put my heart and mind at ease, and God— being the loving Father He is—passed on Reggie's words of comfort to me. After all, I didn't ask to speak with Reggie but God knew how desperately I needed to know my boy was safe in Heaven. I don't have a clear doctrinal explanation of what happened that day, nor do I need one. All I know is that the moment was real, and that God wanted me to be at peace, so He granted me a moment with my son. And for that I will be forever grateful. No one can take this gift from me!

Bundy, however, had great difficulty coming to terms with Reggie's death. He was angry! He couldn't help thinking about how much we had been through, and he began associating God with our hardships, believing He had willfully orchestrated our sorrows. Immediately after Reggie's death Bundy would sometimes feel breathless, so overwhelming was his grief. He often also felt empty, as if he had lost the vital core of his being. It has taken a concerted effort for both Bundy and I to come to terms with Reggie's death. We had to consciously set an intention to grieve, so we could work through this process, rather than grieving passively for the rest of our lives. Bundy is receiving counsel from a traditional bereavement counselor, while I am doing a lot of self-reflection and integrative manual therapy—the same type of hands-on therapy we used on Reggie for three years. We have both agreed to spend the necessary time with our personal support systems, and to talk freely about Reggie. We also decided to turn Reggie's room into a playroom, and have chosen to acknowledge Reggie at family time and holidays. One vitally important aspect of overcoming our grief is to make the choice, every single day, "It is well with my soul."

Bundy and I are not the only people struggling with Reggie's death. Many of the significant figures in our lives are grappling with grief in their own way—my mom and step-dad, my dad, my siblings, my best friend, Heather, Melina, and all the individuals we still refer to as Reggie addicts. Reggie's uncle,

Wayne, went on a drug binge after Reggie's death, and he ended up in jail. It took almost a year, but God used this tragedy to work in Wayne's life and he is doing well. Our beautiful boy left such a vivid impression on such a wide range of utterly different people. The significance of the effect Reggie had on so many people is detailed in the final chapter and, in my humble opinion, this points to the fact that Reggie served his purpose on the Earth.

Chapter Eighteen: Let it Matter

This chapter reveals the unique relationships Reggie developed with a wide range of diverse people, and how our story has on encouraging others to be Mentally STRONG™. As his mom, I am obviously biased, but when you consider the number of people, strangers initially, who drove long distances to be with him, and kept coming back, it's even more obvious Reggie was a rare and special person who was dearly loved by many. The testimonies below bring into clear focus the powerful effect Reggie and the Bundukamara story has had on the lives of those who know us. As you read through these words, think about how to choose to be Mentally STRONG™ and "Let it Matter" in your life. As I place ink to paper in an attempt to convey the life-changing manner in which Reggie has touched and impacted my soul, I know the words I so carefully choose won't do him justice. But accepting and effortlessly rising to the challenge, and doing so with a smile, love, laughter, and on the strength of faith is what being a Bundukamara is all about.

Purpose and Strength--From the Words of Others:

Reggie was born with all the character traits he would need for this life's journey, but we didn't realize it at the time. For one, Reggie is extremely persistent. I quickly learned that childproof absolutely does not mean Reggie-proof! As things got more difficult for him physically, still he persisted. He never gave up. Reggie is passionate. He found his passions at a very early age and nothing would sway him from playing ball, doing everything at a quickened pace and, of course, playing the role of his favorite, friendly, neighborhood masked avenger: Spiderman. Those passions would always give him joy, no matter what. He was born strong and resilient. He would need this strength and called on it daily, he showed us his resilience time and time again, like when he was in the ICU one day and bounced back and was ready for school the next. Reggie taught me how to find these traits within myself. He taught me how to hope even when there was no hope. I am so proud of my Reggie, and for him I am forever grateful.

"If I can quote a song (Matthew 25:21) from my favorite band (Mountain Goats) Reggie, '...you were a presence full of light upon this earth and I am a witness to your life and to it's worth...' I love you and miss you." **Aunt Jada**

"Reggie taught me that at the basis of life what really matters is love. Love is gratitude, gratitude is love. To have a human connection and communication that supersedes all language barriers. To communicate without words and to truly feel and know the energy of love another person gives. Communication through touch-energy. And an appreciation for the person sharing that moment with you."

"Reggie taught me thankfulness and gratitude for the abilities we have, and helped me to *not* feel anger about what could have been. At times I felt frustrated that he couldn't verbally compliment you without blushing, especially if you were a lady, because Reggie certainly was a lady's man!

But in the absence of words, he certainly filled you with love, peace, and laughter!"

―――――――O―――――――

"Seeing and experiencing the pure, innocent, true love Reggie held in his heart, and who he is as a person; I don't know how someone like that doesn't change your life. His *love* for his mother, family, and those there with him sharing that present moment. Nothing made Reggie happier than being around his family and friends, spending time with people and those he loved. He taught me that possessions don't matter, you can't take things with you; relationships and sharing love is what matters. While I am still a work in progress, Reggie taught me the importance of being present in the moment."

―――――――O―――――――

"The whole Bundukamara family is amazing and inspiring, however, they don't see themselves that way. For them this is just life and they take the challenges and hurdles humbly and with love and a smile and faith. Not only Reggie, but the entire Bundukamara family has taught myself and my husband that with Christ and love, you can do *anything*! Doesn't mean there won't be obstacles, and it won't be hard, but with Christ and love, you can do anything and be happy."

"To my Boyfriend: I certainly miss you. You always make me smile. You have placed it on my heart that I feel a calling to minister to the underserved. Every time there is a thunderstorm, my heart is filled at the memory of our time together. Thank you Reggie for the gift of your family, thank you for the time we had together, thank you for impacting my life with you being you. Until we meet again in eternity, all my love.

To Cristi, "You have no idea how much Reggie has impacted me in my heart and my soul. Your son has made me a better person. And for that I am heavenly grateful. And for that I will always be bonded to you and love you. Anytime I think of Reggie I still feel his skin and hair on my fingertips. I wish I had more earthly time with him, but I know that we'll have eternity together. Thank you, Cristi Lynn, and Francis, for giving me the earthly gift of knowing Reggie Josiah. He's an indescribable, amazing soul, an angel! Thank you Jesus for bringing you and I together! You and your family are such a blessing and I love you all!"

Melina, Colorado Reggie Addict

"Reggie was a miracle. Despite many doctors giving him minimal time with us many years ago, he truly left medical personnel in awe and wonder. Reggie wasn't just a miracle, he was a blessing for me and many proud and self-proclaimed Reggie addicts. If you've ever heard me spiel about 'Reggie Therapy' or if I ever dragged you with me, you know how special it was.

Reggie's therapy was unique. All you had to do was sit around him and place your hands on him for an hour or so. You see, Reggie had an extremely rare neurodegenerative disorder that caused him to have a lot of seizure activity. Placing your hands over certain organs allowed Reggie's body to carry out normal and vital processes by diffusing that sporadic electrical activity in those organs. And almost every day for long over three years, all sorts of strangers gathered for one cause.

Initially, everyone thought they were only helping Reggie, but it was clear by one visit that the therapy was our own. Through Reggie, God taught me the meaning of hope in the face of adversity. He taught me that sometimes you just have to take the drive even if the journey is a long one. I learned that serving others doesn't have to be profitable or even opportune to be worth it. I was reminded of the value of family and the gift that is unity. I learned the value and power of touch. I witnessed the relentless love of a mother and father and the joy that comes with that sacrifice. But most of all, God branded my heart with the importance of living a life with purpose and though I'm blue in his absence, I rest in knowing that God's will through Reggie's life was accomplished. Anyone who had the honor of meeting Reggie would agree." **Crystal, Reggie Addict**

——————————O——————————

"The whole family blows my mind. Strongest most inspiring family unit, all held together by Cristi glue. Reggie has a warrior for a mom. God knew what He was doing putting you guys together." **Darla, Reggie Addict**

───────────O───────────

"In August of 2010 I met a boy named Reggie Bundukamara. Standing in that classroom, God told me this boy was going to change the rest of my life. Four years later, myself and a community of impacted people packed him up and watched him move with his family to start a new journey, taking a little piece of my heart with him. The last four months I have watched God continue to use him to touch the lives of others and today, Reggie is in *People* magazine. Not just any *People* magazine, it's the Oscar edition. Reggie, the African boy with a Japanese disorder, who can't speak, has continued to impact so many people without saying a word. He is paving the way for medical science and making an impact in the new community that surrounds him. You can also see him on Weeds 2, March 11th on CNN. I love and miss you guys very much, but I know you're right where God wants you to be. Love you my Rubberband Man." **Ruth, the #1 Reggie Addict**

"Reggie is an inspiration to all of us. I always felt that I was in the presence of an angel whenever I visited him."

"I believe Reggie, Kian, and other brave kids and their families are all fighting to teach us, and are opening new and ground-breaking ways to approach neurological and challenging illnesses so we can fight harder to eliminate them. You and I, my friend, are always going to continue to push through and honor them by fighting harder for this cause. Long live Reggie's love." **Dr Neda Arami MD**

"Dr. B, you and Coach B have always impressed me so much, not only as my former teacher, but as a mother, a mentor and a friend. I cannot put into words how sorry I am for your loss. Reggie was beautiful and his infectious smile I'll never forget. I didn't understand "Reggie Therapy" at first, and I think our time spent with him turned into therapy for all of us, something we looked forward to. Your love for Reggie was fierce and relentless, he couldn't have been any more lucky than to have you both in his corner. Thank you for teaching me more than you'll ever know. My love and sincerest condolences to you and your family at this unbearable time."

"Watching this family fight the good fight for their son with #DRPLA was breath-taking."

"This friendship right here is a God thing for sure! You make me laugh, you challenge me, you *amaze* me, and teach me so much about life! You are one of my *heroes* in life! I'm thankful to call you friend! Thank you for being vulnerable. Thank you for letting me learn some of the greatest lessons I have ever gained, by watching you put one foot in front of the other these last months. To learn ultimately that grief is praise. And that the only way to get through it is to #letitmatter—your entire family is amazing. And you're amazing even when you don't feel like you are! I will be your arm bearer! All my love and prayers for peace!" **Heather, CEO Realm of Caring**

💜 Reggie filled our hearts and souls with his strength and determination. I loved to hold his hand and he would give me a squeeze. He was a beautiful boy and we are so blessed to have had him in our lives. He inspired many. Thank you for sharing him with us, as he is our child too. We love him and we love all of you. Sending love and hugs during this heart-breaking time."

"He stole our hearts forever!" **Alex, Reggie Addict**

"Child of God whose spirit and influence was felt across the globe."

"Reggie's life matters, it touched everyone who met him. It made everyone who met him better in some way. Your family continues to touch the world, Cristi, with your faith, *hope*, dignity, power, love, perseverance, kindness, selflessness, resilience, and I could go on and on. It's an honor to have been part of the Bundy story! You are loved today more than any other day." **Stacy, YFC missionary**

"Thank you for being part of my search for the truth..."

"Cristi, since the moment I met you I knew you were special. Your energy, your contagious laughter, your passion to teach, and just your awesome presence itself was great to be around. And then... I learned more about you and your life, struggles, and faith, and it made me look at you in awe... To see this woman with so many difficult obstacles and trials in front of her, yet filled with so much life. I knew you were one of God's special angels on Earth. And I know He must see the strength of a warrior when He looks at you. Otherwise, He would never give you so many challenges. I know this is a bittersweet compliment from God because you don't want to be a warrior—you want to be with your babies. But I am so happy that Reggie had a mother like you, someone who was always filled with love and faith and hope, and with the relentless drive of a true mother, willing to do anything and everything to save her family. You even relocated your family across the country, and faced a lot of controversy in order to save your son. You are an amazing woman that I will never forget. You are *exactly* what I picture when I think of the kind of mother I pray to be to my new son, and the kind of follower of Christ who, despite the surrounding situation, still clings to His word, even though the doubt, fear, and pain. You are forever imprinted in my mind as a perfect role model to follow, and an excellent example of unconditional love. I have not seen you in over four years, and I was only your student for a short while, but the impact you have made on my life is extraordinary, and I will always have you and your family in my heart and mind. Thank you for allowing me to put my hands on Reggie for his treatments, for bringing me into your home, and laying plain for me to see what a woman of God can overcome while still being a blessing to others. **Sasha, Reggie Addict**

"Thank you for allowing me to pray over Reggie. I'll never forget the day he smiled at me—it filled my heart with so much joy; he was truly special. And thank you for always making me feel special, choosing my hands to go over his most precious organ, his heart. I always felt a connection with you. Please never apologize again for being the kind of mother you are and for never giving up the fight and giving it your all. Don't be sorry for having faith and dedicating him to God, because He truly was used by God to change the world. And don't ever apologize for not saying bye, because this is not goodbye, it is only, 'see you soon my love.'"

"I believe in life there are words no child should have to hear; seizures, palliative care, quality of life, terminal illness. But this is the reality so many children and their families face. Grief is something that no matter how hard you try or how well prepared you think you are, when it washes over you it's a tidal wave. Dr. B tells me she's not good with words, but I think she has opened her heart and shared something so profound, in such a way, with open vulnerability. Today we remember a brave fighter on what would have been his eighteenth birthday."

"Dr. B, it has been many years since you welcomed me into your home to help with Reggie's therapies. I never knew the power such a wonderful young boy could have on my life. He had an infectious smile that just warmed your heart. My heart and prayers go out to you and your family to help ease the pain I heard in your video. You are such an inspirational woman and you have touched the lives of so many people with your knowledge, courage, and the immense love you radiate. You are such an amazing person. I pray you find the strength to truly believe you are the best mother a child can have. Reggie was very lucky to have you fighting for him with every breath."

"Reggie taught me how to suffer like a man"

Grandpa West

89418616R00146

Made in the USA
Middletown, DE
16 September 2018